I0816101

MG MIDGETS
In Detail

MG MIDGETS
In Detail

BY MALCOLM GREEN

Herridge & Sons

Acknowledgements

This book could not have been written or illustrated without help from a great many people. Firstly I must thank all the owners of the MGs I have photographed and I would particularly like to mention the following, some sadly no longer with us. If due to memory fade I have missed out anyone, I can only apologise.

Sheila and Colin Ballard, Christopher Banton, John Bates, Philip and Rosemary Bayne-Powell, Michael Bean, Jerry Birkbeck, Chris Blood, Neill Bruce, Pam and John Butler, Michael and Andrea Card, Roger Chamberlain, Chris Collingham, Dave Cooksey, Martin Curren, Mike Dalby, Les Deykin, Bryan Ditchman, Iain and Rose Evans, Barry Foster, Patrick Gardner, Jon Goddard, Ted Hack, Keith Hall, Alan Hogg, Nicky and Terry Holden, David Hutchison, Angie and Andy King, Mike Long, Richard Meere, Hiro Nishio, Oliver Richardson, Malcolm Sockett, Barry Walker, Brian Wigg. I must also say that I used the very useful information in *Maintaining the Breed* by John Thornley and for compiling the specification panels *The Magic of the Marque* by Mike Allison.

Last, but certainly not least, I must thank my wife, Andrea as without her help and encouragement, plus her skill in researching the finer details of automotive history, it is unlikely that this or any of my previous books would have seen the light of day.

Malcolm Green
Shropshire 2024

Published 2024 by
Herridge & Sons Ltd
Lower Forda, Shebbear
Beaworthy,
Devon EX21 5SY

ISBN 978-1-914929-11-3
Printed in China

Contents

Introduction

Although this book concentrates on the MG Midgets built from 1928 to 1955, we included this short account of the development of the Company prior to then for those readers unfamiliar with the early years of the MG brand.

Firstly, it is certain that no MGs of any type would have been built without William Morris, later Lord Nuffield, first establishing Morris Motors and building Morris cars. William possessed a mechanical aptitude and initially learned to ride on a borrowed penny-farthing. When he was fourteen he bought his first bicycle, a so-called safety cycle with solid tyres. This machine he frequently stripped and rebuilt and this activity was to teach him a lot about how bicycles were built and worked. Having abandoned his first choice of career in medicine, because of a need to start earning, he went to work for a bicycle repairer. However, he soon left that job and with capital of just £4.00 went into business on his own. Working from his father's house and with the front room there as a showroom, he soon built a good following locally as a bicycle repairer. His reputation was also enhanced by success as a cycle racer and by 1900 he held seven local championships.

As work increased he moved the showroom to rented premises at 48 High Street, Oxford and the workshop and storage to nearby 1 Queen Street. The move towards mechanical transport came in 1902 when he built a motorcycle powered by an engine he built using ready-made castings. This was a success and he and Joseph Cooper went into partnership to sell, service and make motorcycles. They took on premises in Longwall and the venture was a success, but the partnership did not survive a difference of opinion between the two men. Another partnership followed but this too was a failure and ended twelve months later leaving William

The combination of the Morris Garages body and the modified Morris rolling chassis created an extremely attractive car.

with a £50 debt. He decided that in future he would never go into business with anyone else.

Once he also began repairing cars, the motorcycle premises proved useful for storing cars that were in for repair. By 1903 he had another business, offering a taxi service and cars for hire. In 1910 increasing trade needed more space and the Longwall Street premises were rebuilt and the business became The Morris Garage, later changed to The Morris Garages as more premises were acquired. The garage was also agent for many cars, like Humber, Singer, Standard and Wolseley. The next step was to move to building his own car and at the 1912 London Motor Show he announced that next year the first Morris car would be produced. He issued a detailed specification and this tempted dealers Stewart and Arden to place an advance order for 400 cars. They later were appointed Morris main dealers for the London area.

One incentive for his efforts was the success of imported Model A Fords. Ever keen to promote British manufacturers, Morris thought there should be a local volume car producer. Having gained experience dealing with customer's preferences and of the service requirements of various makes of car he tried to design his car to meet these. He purchased the majority of components from outside suppliers and acquired a disused training college at Cowley as his factory. Although the first Morris was not the cheapest car on the market, it soon gained a reputation for its strength and earned awards in reliability trials. The first Morris Oxfords used 8.9hp White & Poppe engines, but by the time of the 1913 Motor Show there were many improvements and a closed model joined the range. The 1915 model Morris Cowley shown to the press late in 1914 had an 11.9hp American Continental engine and American axles, gearbox and steering gear. The outbreak of war eventually stopped Morris production and his factory went over to supplying military items for the armed forces.

When the armistice was declared in 1918 there was an initial boom in car sales with the price of the Morris Oxford 2-seater raised to £535. By 1921 sales were falling and prices were cut by £25 and by the time of the Motor Show that autumn the price was down to £415, with similar reductions for other models in the range. As with other manufacturers at that time, Morris sold cars as rolling chassis, as well as complete off-the-shelf models. This allowed customers and dealers who wanted closed cars to have them finished by outside coachbuilders. In 1924 Morris added a saloon model to the range. Continental pattern engines were still used, but were now made in England in a factory that had been used by Hotchkiss et Cie for military work, but was now redundant and unused. However the person who was most responsible for bringing MG cars into existence was Cecil Kimber. In 1921 William Morris had appointed him sales manager of Morris Garages in the hope he could deal with a difficult trading environment.

Cecil Kimber was born in 1888 into a comfortably well off family. They lived in Dulwich, then a growing and fashionable area, and the family firm of Hughes & Kimber had exhibited their innovative copper and steel printing plates at the 1855 Paris Exhibition. In 1896 Henry Kimber and his brother Walter opened a separate printing supplies business in Manchester and this meant the family had to move to Stockport. Cecil then went to Stockport Grammar School and on leaving there went to work for his father at the

A booklet created around the time of the 1928 London Motor Show giving details of the 18/80, 14/40 and Midget models.

supplies company. He also attended evening classes at Manchester Technical School.

Cecil had developed an interest in motorcycles and would cycle long distances to see them ridden in time trials and other events. In 1906 Cecil was able to buy his first motorcycle, a single-cylinder Rex. He had joined the Warrington and District Motor Club and started to enter Club events, in 1907 exchanging his Rex for the more powerful twin-cylinder version. All this came to an end one day when he was riding a friend's motorcycle and was hit by a car, with life-changing consequences. His right thigh and leg was so damaged that at first the hospital wanted to perform an amputation. Luckily they opted to save the leg, but this meant a series of operations over the following years and in the end left him with one leg shorter than the other.

As the accident was the fault of the other driver, he was awarded £700 compensation, around £110,000 today, and using some of this bought his first car, a 10hp Singer. He continued to work for his father earning just one pound a week. As he by then had met and married Rene Hunt he asked for a raise, but this was refused. Instead his father wanted the balance of the compensation money for the business. Cecil would not agree to this and resigned. The pair parted on bad terms and for the rest of his life Henry would not even speak to his son. Obviously then needing a job, Cecil joined Sheffield-Simplex as personal assistant to their Chief Engineer. In1916 they moved to Surrey when Kimber took the post as buyer for AC Cars in Thames Ditton, with Rene as his secretary. He returned to Birmingham in 1918 to join E.G. Wrigley Limited who in 1913 had moved to new premises and for a few months built their own car.

The standard 18/80 models on offer at launch.

After the fighting stopped in 1918, that company supplied components for a new venture established in empty premises at Birtley, Tyne and Weir by Sir William Sanderson Company. Kimber had money in this enterprise that he lost when it later collapsed. William , in a probable attempt to recover the cost of those parts he had supplied, purchased the assets from the liquidator. Prior to that, William Morris had offered Kimber a job at Morris Garages. This was a business separate from the car building Morris Motors and unlike that company was still owned solely by William Morris.

The Morris Garages staff under Armstead in the Queen Street, Oxford showroom prior to Kimber's arrival consisted of two drivers for the car hire side of the business, one of them when needed could help out the full-time salesman. There was also a man dealing with counter sales of parts, etc. In addition one lady manned the switchboard and another was the secretary. Around the corner from the showroom was a yard behind the Clarendon Hotel that Morris took over to use as workshops. Here one of the mechanics in the section dealing with motorcycle repairs was Cecil Cousins, he would later play a vital role in the MG story.

Another man who went on to be the brains behind so many of the record-breaking achievements and new road cars was Albert Sydney (Syd) Enever. Taken on aged fourteen as the odd-job boy, Syd spent his first year cleaning and moving cars in the showroom as well as riding a bicycle fitted with a basket and Morris Garages signs to take messages and small parts between the Morris Garages premises and also to and from the Morris factory at Cowley. After this he was moved into the workshop to train as a mechanic. When he was sixteen he was taught to drive and used an old Morris Cowley to collect parts from Cowley. This car was later fitted with a van body painted with Morris Garages signs and used for moving parts between premises.

In March 1922 Edward Armstead resigned and a temporary replacement was put in place. Armstead later committed suicide. As his permanent replacement, Morris appointed Cecil Kimber, someone he thought had the energy and enthusiasm needed for the job. All the necessary people to see the start of the MG marque were now in place. As this was a difficult time for sales Kimber attempted to widen their market by offering cars that were not readily available from other dealers. This initially proved successful. A Morris Cowley built to order for customers and given Chummy bodywork by Carbodies of Coventry was popular until Morris Motors brought in for the 1924 model year a similar car at a lower price. The Morris Garages cars had been completed in the Clarendon workshops, putting pressure on the available space.

In another exercise, Kimber had six Morris chassis collected from Cowley. These had any faults revealed in road tests corrected and were then given bodywork made by the local coachbuilder, Raworth. Offered as Morris Garages Chummy at £350, they proved very slow to sell with customers going for the standard Morris model when these were available. The Morris Garages cars were assembled in the Longwall Street premises. Unfortunately they sold slowly as they were expensive and the introduction for the 1934 model year at of a Morris Chummy a lower price did not help. Kimber saw that to sell cars already fitted with their coachwork they needed to add exclusive features, like improved performance. It is also true that special badging could help and it is significant that the first use of the MG octagon was in an advert in the November 1923 issue of *The Isis*.

Details of the extra carrying space when using the lowered boot lid on the 18/80 saloons.

The first cars that could be seen as being special enough to qualify as MGs were the Morris Garages Super Sports models announced late in 1923 for sale in 1924. This indeed signals the start of MG as a distinct brand. A new car fitted with a Kimber designed saloon body with a V-shaped windscreen, based on the 14/28 Morris Oxford Chassis and priced at £460, was advertised in the March 1924 issue of *The Morris Owner*. In following issues of the same magazine other body styles were illustrated. The Morris Oxford was modified late in 1924, with the changes including better brakes and a longer chassis. These improvements were incorporated in the 14/28 MG with these cars also receiving further improvements to the steering, suspension and controls at Alfred Lane before being fitted with their smart coachwork. The MG Super Sports range comprised an open four-seater, an open two-seater and a two-door Salonette at prices from £350 to £475. The Morris Garages continued to offer special bodywork on unmodified Morris chassis at lower prices.

Kimber entered a modified Chummy in the 1923 Land's End Trial and won a gold medal, so he decided to enter a specially built car in the 1925 event. An OHV Hotchkiss engine was obtained, stripped and modified. A special chassis was constructed from altered Morris Cowley components and fitted with a modified braking system constructed from many special parts made in the little machine shop at Longwall Street. Fitted with a purposeful looking two-seater body manufactured by Carbodies, when tested by Kimber the car was reputed to have been capable of reaching a top speed of 82mph. Accompanied by Oxford insurance broker Wilfred Mathews, Kimber had a trouble free run, gaining a gold medal for their efforts. This car is now celebrated as Old Number One.

By September 1925, the space available at Alfred

14/40 Mark IV was available as 2- & 4-seater tourers as well as 2- & 4-door saloon models.

Lane was proving insufficient to cope with the numbers of cars being built. The Morris Garages rented a section of a new radiator factory in Bainton Road, Oxford with MG production being transferred there. The catalogue of 1926 MG models was a much more professional affair than those previously issued by The Morris Garages. Inside the front cover was the proud statement that such is the popularity of the various MG models that a special factory has been erected to cope with the ever-increasing demand. The MG had now established a place in the market as a product that differed distinctly from the Morris cars on which they were based. A combination of some simple chassis modifications and more attractive bodywork had transformed the mundane Morris Oxford into a much better machine that could compete on equal terms with other makes of sporting cars. Around 400 examples of the bullnose radiator 14/28 MGs had been built before a radical re-design of the parent car was announced in September 1926, bringing production of this most elegant of vintage cars to a close.

The new Morris Oxford chassis was wider, shorter and much heavier than its predecessor and was now fitted with a flat radiator in place of the familiar rounded design that had been a distinctive Morris trademark, and one that had blended well with the elegant MG body styles. Modifying the chassis and designing new bodies to fit caused Kimber a number of problems and he resorted to asking for assistance from a young engineering graduate, H.N. Charles. He persuaded Charles to join his team at Bainton Road at the weekends to sort out what was necessary to get the MG range back into production and they spent long periods working on sketches trying to adapt the body styles to suit the flat radiator.

The new models that were eventually put into production featured a number of chassis and brake modifications in an effort to improve on the Morris chassis. The range of body styles was essentially as previously available, two- and four-seater open tourers and two- and four-seater two-door Salonettes, but a heavy four-door saloon body was no longer listed. These first cars on the new chassis are now known as 14/28 Flat-nose, to distinguish them from the earlier 14/28s. Development work continued, resulting in various modifications being incorporated into the car which was eventually called the 14/40 Mark IV.

Early in 1927 the MG lines were moved to a new

14/28 flat radiator two-seater photographed in a London street.

section of the works as radiator production was growing apace, matching an increase in sales of Morris cars. It was obvious that new premises would eventually be needed to accommodate the car assembly work, so Cecil Kimber approached William Morris for permission to have a separate factory built especially for MG production. The go-ahead was given, and work commenced on new buildings in Edmund Road, Cowley where they were close to the Morris works with easy access to the bulk of their components.

The new factory had an eight-bay assembly area and production was moved from Bainton Road in September 1927. Morris Garages now had a modern factory in which to build their cars. A production line was laid down for chassis assembly, stores were established to serve both the assembly lines and provide customer service, and a small part of the factory was set aside for the engine tuning work to be carried out. A special running-in bay was installed where completed chassis had their engines connected to a supply of coal gas to provide fuel, and to a water supply for cooling, before being run for the equivalent of 750 miles. The chassis was then taken back to the main assembly area where the head was removed and de-carbonized and the valves reground. The wings and valances, bulkhead, fuel tank, etc. were then attached to make the car roadworthy for a test drive. Brake and shock absorber settings were adjusted and the car returned to the works for running on a test rig designed by Hubert (H.N.) Charles, which was the equivalent of a modern rolling road. A temporary seat was then installed for its journey by road to the coachbuilders where the body was fitted. Upon its return the final small fittings were added and the car readied for sale.

In an effort to take the Morris cars up-market, it was decided that an entirely new six-cylinder engine be designed. Initially this was installed in an unsuitable chassis, but Cecil Kimber still wanted the engine for an MG so he set about having a new

The attractive setting for this flat radiator 14/28 two-seater tourer is probably in one of the villages near Oxford.

This MG 14/40 with a four-seater body can be identified from the earlier model by the apron added below the radiator.

An MG 14/40 with a Gordon England body built using their patented method of having metal plates to link the wooden timbers, while holding them apart from each other. This was done to reduce creaks and rattles from them as the chassis twisted over bumps in the road. This car was at one time the factory hack, called Old Speckled Hen, and from 1979 this was also the name given to a locally brewed beer.

frame drawn up and produced which incorporated all the features he required. The result was a strong chassis with suspension and steering able to cope with the power output of the 2468cc six-cylinder engine. The standard of construction was very high and the cast aluminium bulkhead, incorporating the MG octagon in the side brackets, was a work of art. The most imposing feature of the MG Six, as it was called, was the new radiator. No longer did the car have to suffer a standard Morris item fitted with an MG badge, for the 18/80 a special radiator was designed with a handsome polished surround and with the MG octagon sitting on a crest-shaped nosepiece. This design would adorn all subsequent production MGs until the TF was announced in 1953.

In 1928, for the first time, The MG Car Company had taken its own stand at the London Motor Show held at Olympia each autumn. Such was the reception for the new MG when it was launched at this show, and when it was road-tested by the motoring press, that Kimber was certain he was going to sell large numbers of them. Unfortunately the car was much more expensive than the previous model, with the chassis-only price rising by fifty per cent from £280 for the 14/40 to £420 for the 18/80, while the cost of a completed two-seater climbed from £335 to £480. Although the car was to sell well initially, the poor economic climate following the stock market crash in the USA and subsequent worldwide depression, meant that the numbers of potential buyers for such a large and expensive car were dwindling. However, the fortunes of MG as a marque were to survive this setback almost entirely due to the announcement at the same show of a completely different type of MG, The 8/33, or M-type, Midget.

An attractive 18/80 fitted with a two-seater body.

The M-Type Midget

The first MG Midgets left the Morris Garages assembly lines in 1929 to establish a new breed of small British sports cars that over the following years came to dominate their section of the market. It is difficult to overstate the importance of that model to the subsequent development of the marque, but it is possible that without the introduction of an affordable sports model the MG name may not have survived beyond the early 1930s. Remember that when the M-type was announced towards the end of 1928 the previously available MG models were up-market versions of the Morris Oxford that sold for prices well over double that of the new Midget. The new Quick Six, the18/80, was even more expensive. Customers for these larger cars were necessarily reasonably wealthy and sales were thus fairly limited. These more affluent people were often the most affected by a collapse in share prices, leading to a drop in their income.

The decision taken in 1928 by Cecil Kimber to build a small sports car based on the just-conceived Morris Minor is now seen as of great importance, but at the time the success of the venture was probably not a foregone conclusion and was, perhaps, something of a leap in the dark. The expansion of the marque by 1927, from Morris Garages fitting a few Morris chassis with their design of coachwork, to having a purpose-built factory in Edmund Road, Oxford, dedicated to assembling the MG 14/40 Super Sports models, was a remarkable achievement. On the other hand, the economic climate following the Wall Street Crash in October 1929 was not at all promising, and even those not affected were less inclined to flaunt their wealth at a time when many were out of work. For the 1930 season onwards sales of expensive cars were likely to suffer.

This advert was placed in the special issues of the major magazines to direct visitors to see the new MG Midget on the Morris stand at the 1928 London Motor Show at Olympia. The car on show was one of the prototypes with a flared scuttle.

That decision to build the Midget may not have been taken by Kimber alone as at that time William Morris owned Morris Garages privately and played an active part in the running of the company as well as with Morris Motors. He had seen the huge impact on the market created by the Austin Seven and was probably keen not only have a suitable Morris in his range, but also to have a product from his MG specialist car company to rival the sporting versions of that successful small car. Whoever it was who then had the foresight to design and build a miniature sports car based on the chassis of the just announced Morris Minor, read the market well. There is little doubt that had a more affordable alternative not

A feature of the early cars was the rear-hinged doors and the front brake levers coming through the side panels. This is one of the prototype cars and many changes were made before full production began.

The dashboard of an early car built in Oxford.

The front brake operating mechanism protruding through the side panel was a feature of the M-types built in Oxford.

been available to the relatively expensive MG 18/80 model launched at the same time as the Midget, then the marque would have faded into obscurity within a very few years. Actually the 1929 model year was a high point as the 18/80s and Midgets sold well, with around 290 of the larger cars and about 500 Midgets leaving the factory.

Promoted as a full-size car in miniature, the Austin Seven had been launched in 1923 and its design had virtually wiped out the opposition from the quirky and unreliable cyclecars that had previously provided budget motoring. Sports models had been available from 1924 and these were successful: the Brooklands Super Sports at £265 came with a certificated top speed of 75mph. Several firms offered special sporting coachwork for the lightweight chassis with its quarter-elliptic rear springing. In the 750cc classes the Austin Seven was to prove to be a rival for MG on both the track and in record breaking.

Morris, on the other hand, had relied for most of the 1920s on variations of his successful bullnose design, the smallest capacity engine of which was rated at 11.9hp. In an era when road tax was calculated by bore size under the RAC system, the lack of a 7hp car to rival the Austin Seven was a disadvantage. When the acquisition by Morris in 1927 of the bankrupt Wolseley Motors gave him access to sufficient talent and capacity to design and build a small OHC power unit, this was the opportunity to produce a much-needed entry model for the Morris range.

The simple chassis for the Morris Minor had half-elliptic springs all round, a 78-inch wheelbase and a 42-inch track. The four-cylinder engine had a bore of 57mm and a stroke of 83mm, giving a capacity of 847cc, 100cc greater than the contemporary Austin Seven. The treasury rating was 8hp, resulting in an annual tax of £8. Among those responsible for the engine was Oliver Boden. He had been Works Manager at Wolseley when Morris purchased the company in 1927 and was retained in the same role under the new ownership. His name and that of Wolseley appear on the patent for the vertical dynamo improvements for the Minor engine. However, one has to look further back to trace the origins of the design, as the Wolseley Company had used many of its features in previous power units. The most obvious of these was having a vertical drive to provide a gear-driven link between the crankshaft and the camshaft. Rockers transferred lift for the valves from the camshaft to the heads of the valve stems. On the Minor/Midget engine the vertical drive was taken through the dynamo, causing the oil leaks and charging problems encountered by generations of MG owners. Wolseley dropped the vertical dynamo

A batch of M-type Midgets in the Morris Garages Clarendon Yard premises in Oxford await delivery to customers.

and a sidevalve engine was designed for the Minor and fitted to cars built from the beginning of 1931.

The Morris Minor appeared at the 1928 Motor Show in two forms, a fabric-covered two-door, four-seater saloon of lightweight construction and a four-seater tourer. The saloon cost £135 and the open car £125. One of two prototype MG Midgets shared the limelight with the Minor at that 1928 Motor Show, without an engine installed. The second car was running and served as a demonstrator. It is just possible that these two cars were built to test the market before committing to full production. There is evidence that the original intention was for both the Minor and the MG to have 7hp engines to compete directly with the Austin Seven. The change to bore size to take the engine into the 8hp bracket was made at a late stage, perhaps because of poor performance of the prototypes on test.

The work on the Minor chassis to convert it from a Morris to an MG followed a pattern established by Kimber for previous models. The springs were flattened, the steering column set at a lower angle, the gear lever re-shaped and the foot pedals altered. To set the whole car off, a smaller version of the MG radiator that had been designed for the 18/80 headed

MG

The M.G. Midget Sports

Mk. I.

THERE are many to whom the fascination of a sports car makes a strong appeal, but who have hitherto been unable to afford the purchase and maintenance costs necessary to gratify their ambition ; others, while able to afford a large car would prefer a " baby " for its handiness and ease of control, but are unwilling to sacrifice the road worthiness and comfort of the heavyweight. To these, and to every sporting motorist with appreciation for high class design, the M.G. Midget makes its appeal.

Because its engine is small, the tax is only £8 per annum, the petrol consumption 40—50 m.p.g. and other running costs proportionately low. Because its engine is a highly efficient overhead camshaft unit—no experiment, but the outcome of years of experience and trial—its performance is high, and it will hum up to the fifties and sixties without effort and without fuss.

And, most important of all, its low chassis frame, upswept fore and aft and carried on flat semi-elliptic springs, is of the real " big car " type, so that with all its light weight it possesses road holding qualities hitherto unrealised in so small a chassis.

Sole Manufacturers :

The M.G. Car Company

Proprietors : The Morris Garages Ltd.

Phone 2241 **Oxford** Wire : " Auto "

The single-page flyer for the Midget distributed from the MG stand at the 1928 London Motor Show.

The M.G. Midget Sports £175

Body Finishes.

Pillar-box Red or Cerulean Blue fabric exterior with Black leather cloth pneumatic upholstery. Wings, wheels and chassis Black cellulose.

THE rear locker is exposed by lifting the hinged lid of the tail. In this space is housed the spare wheel firmly secured to the floor. The hood and hood sticks—which although completely detachable are very easily erected—are carried in a pocket and clips in the lid itself. The remainder of the space is available for luggage. Tools are carried in a separate compartment in the tail.

The M.G. Car Company. Oxford.

MG

The 8/33 M.G. Midget Sports.

"HOLDS the road like a leech at 60 m.p.h." This was said recently of the 8/33 M.G. Midget Sports which weighs just ten cwt. It sounds incredible but it is only to be expected when the facts are known. This car is designed and produced by specialists in a model factory from which nothing but M.G. Sports Cars emanate. The chassis is modelled upon that of the larger M.G. Sports, being upswept front and rear with long flat semi-elliptic springs, hence the wonderful road holding qualities. The overhead valve engine is capable of attaining and maintaining a very high speed.

The attractive stream-lined two seater body completes this wonderful little sports car which is indeed "built like a big car."

CHASSIS SPECIFICATION.

General. The design consists basically of a four cylinder water cooled overhead camshaft engine with unit construction clutch and three speed gearbox, mounted in a sturdy frame carried on semi-elliptic springs.

Engine. The engine is 8.05 h.p. Treasury Rating, Tax £8 per annum, with bore and stroke of 57 mm. and 83 mm. respectively, giving a cubic capacity of 847 c.c. The four cylinders and practically the whole of the crankcase form one rigid casting, and provide a stout support for the exceptionally sturdy two bearing crankshaft. The overhead valves are operated through rocker fingers by an overhead camshaft carried on the detachable cylinder head. Valve adjustment by eccentric bush. At the front end of the crankshaft is a bevel drive to a vertical spindle which also forms the armature shaft of the dynamo, this last being vertically mounted on a cylinder block casting. Above the dynamo, the drive is taken through a flexible universal metal joint to the half-time gear and the camshaft. This position for the dynamo obviates backlash and noise in the camshaft driving gear. Two ring aluminium pistons and duralumin connecting rods are fitted. The induction pipe and exhaust manifold are both on the near side of the engine.

Carburetter. S.U. automatic piston type carburetter is fitted, with hand throttle and mixture controls on the dash.

Lubrication. Pressure lubrication is used throughout, the oil pump, which is submerged, supplying the main bearings, big ends, valve gear and distribution gear.

Cooling. Cooling is by thermo-syphon, aided by a two blade belt driven fan. The radiator, of entirely new M.G. design, is of the film type, and the casing is solid nickel.

Transmission. The clutch and gearbox assembly are built in unit with the engine, the former being of the single dry plate type. The gearbox provides three speeds forward and reverse, with direct drive on top, and control is effected by a central lever, which is cranked well back and provides very easy gear changing without groping or stretching. The ratios are:

Top: 4.89—1. Bottom: 17—1.
Second: 8.96—1. Reverse: 13.83—1

At 1,000 engine revolutions per minute, the speeds on the forward gears are approximately:

Bottom gear: 4.7 m.p.h.
Second gear: 9.0 m.p.h.
Top gear: 16.5 m.p.h.

From the gearbox the drive is taken to the three-quarter floating type spiral bevel rear axle by an open propeller shaft, at each end of which is a Hardy disc universal joint.

Chassis Frame. The chassis frame is exceptionally robust. It is tapered, and upswept front and rear, while there are five cross members to ensure rigidity.

Springs. Long flat semi-elliptic springs are employed fore and aft, and in conjunction with the upswept chassis frame, provide a very low centre of gravity and excellent road holding.

Shock Absorbers. The road springs are checked by adjustable Hartford shock absorbers.

Steering. The steering, which is of the worm and wheel type, is finger light at all speeds, and the column is simply adjustable for rake.

Electrical. Ignition is by Lucas 6-volt coil and battery, the distributor being driven by skew gearing from the crankshaft, and inclined outwards, so that it is instantly accessible. As explained above, the dynamo is interposed into the overhead camshaft drive, and the starter motor, of the gear type, is spigoted into the flywheel casing. An electric horn, large headlamps, side lamps, and tail lamp are included in the specification.

Brakes. The foot brake operates on all four wheels, and the brakes are of the two-shoe type operated by rods and cables. From the pedal, a rod, which incorporates a single point adjustment, is connected to a lever on the brake cross shaft. This cross shaft, which is very stout and carried in three bearings, has double levers at each end from which rods and cables operate direct on the four wheels. There are also individual adjustments for each wheel, and the whole system provides smooth, powerful braking, with automatic compensation by wear. The hand lever, which is centrally disposed, operates contracting shoes in a brake drum situated aft of the gearbox. This provides an entirely independent parking brake, and entirely satisfies the law regarding "two independent brakes."

Petrol System. A 4½ gallon petrol tank is carried in the dash, feeding by gravity to the carburettor through a two-way tap operated from inside the car, which provides a reserve of approximately one gallon.

Instruments. The instrument panel incorporates: 80 m.p.h. speedometer, oil gauge, ammeter and switches.

Wheels. Five wire wheels, of the three stud fixing type, with Dunlop 27in. x 4.00in. balloon tyres, are included.

NOTE.—*The right is reserved to vary the above specification without notice.*

The M.G. Car Company. Oxford.

The booklet issued at the 1928 show to serious customers for any of the MG models had two pages devoted to the Midget.

a fabric-covered two-seater body, two of which had been ordered from Carbodies of Coventry. The first order was dated 6th September 1928 and the second 22nd September; both were for what was described as a Morris Minor two-seater sports (Midget). Although an entirely new concept in small sporting cars, the Midget attracted a lot of attention at Olympia and this provided around 200 orders. With such public acceptance of the new MG, Kimber went ahead and placed an order with Carbodies for 498 bodies, these being of a revised design that replaced the swept-up scuttle seen on the show cars with one that was completely flat. The order represented then the largest number of bodies ever supplied to MG.

At the 1928 Motor Show, stands in the main hall only went to companies building complete cars, and the MG cars were still considered to be part of Morris, so the new MG Midget and 18/80 were on show as part of the much larger Morris exhibit. The September 1928 preview in *The Autocar* of the next year's models, in describing the new MG, particularly noted the low seating position, the lack of the then almost universal running boards and the neat design of the fabric-covered body. They anticipated its popularity with those keen on motor sport, especially as the price was expected to be very competitive.

Despite the strong market for MG cars at that time, an expected change during 1929 was the subject of an article in the following issue of the same magazine. The writer anticipated that the smaller cars then appearing would become very popular, but suggested that this would not increase congestion as they would not take up a lot of room on the road. Not everyone applauded the arrival of lighter, smaller cars. It was as a reaction to these buzz-boxes, as they called them, that a group of owners of the more traditional sporting cars, like Alvis, Bentley, Lagonda, etc., in 1934 formed the Vintage Sports-Car Club with a cut-off date for eligibility being the end of December 1930. The fact that this would eventually make them accept cars like the early Midget and Austin Sevens as true vintage cars is rather ironic.

Cecil Kimber was reluctant to commit to building cars without some guaranteed orders. So it is not surprising that it was only after seeing the reception accorded by dealers and public to the Midget at the show that steps were made to begin building the cars. In the event, it was not until March 1929 that a production line was established at the MG factory in Edmund Road, Oxford. Even at that time, so popular was the new MG that there was insufficient room there for cars to be fully finished. At this stage the rolling chassis were towed from the Morris works

A well-used example of an M-type body built at Abingdon. It has front-hinged doors and cable-operated brakes concealed behind the side valances.

at Cowley to Edmund Road for conversion to MG specification and for the body to be fitted. However, so limited was the space in the assembly area that the cars were then moved to the Morris Garages premises in Leopold Street for painting and for the wings and bonnet to be assembled. The cars then returned to Edmund Road for final inspection before despatch to dealers and distributors.

The initial press reports were written largely from copy provided to journalists as there had been no opportunity for them to try out the new model. *The Autocar*, in their issue of 14th September 1928, had a couple of photographs of the car and a full description, and said that the new model was 'likely to become popular with the sporting kind of motorist, particularly in view of the expected moderate price'. The same magazine, in their motor show issue the following month, said 'the MG Midget would make small sports car history'. The October/November 1928 issue of the cash-strapped *Motor Sport* magazine carried details of the 1929 MG programme, and of the Midget they said that here at last was the real sports car in miniature; a car with real performance at little more than motorcycle cost.

The earliest sales brochures produced to help sell the M-type described the new model as 'The MG Midget Sports Mark 1' and was illustrated with an attractive drawing of the car by Leslie Grimes picturing the car on an airfield with hangers and aircraft in the background and a young lady wearing a cloche hat standing alongside the red car. The brochure emphasised the virtues of the small engine, tax was only £8 per annum, petrol consumption 40 to 50mpg, and other running costs proportionally low. This leaflet also listed the colours available as red or light blue fabric, with the bonnet, valances and wheels cellulosed to match and the wings painted black. This and other contemporary advertising material showed cars with flared scuttles.

An Abingdon-built car with a metal-covered body tub.

The first full road test of the Midget appeared in *The Light Car and Cyclecar* in May 1929. They opened their report with the comment, 'The 8/33 MG Midget can be summed up by saying that it is a thoroughbred little sports car, and that implies a great deal'. The magazine tried out two cars, finding that each had almost identical performance. It is surprising that they fell for the ruse adopted by Kimber when he called the model the 8/33 Midget and said that the car had 33bhp when it was more like 20. They recorded a top speed of 63mph. *The Motor* described their test vehicle as a fascinating small car with exceptionally good performance and obtained a maximum speed of 65mph. At Brooklands they took the car up the test hill and found that it tackled the maximum gradient of 1 in 4 with ease. They thought the MG Midget filled a real niche in the sports car world and was capable of holding its own with any other cars of a similar type.

With sales of both the Midget and the 18/80 well above expectations, the limitations of the space at the Edmund Road factory were a real problem. With the blessing of Morris, Kimber searched for new premises and found the answer to be a section of the Pavlova Leather works in Abingdon that had not been used since 1919. After strenuous efforts to clear out unused equipment and the vats used in the tanning process, plus re-laying the concrete floors, production moved to the new premises towards the end of 1929, just in time for the financial downturn to drastically reduce demand for more expensive cars, like the 18/80 and the new Mark II version being developed.

Prior to the start of production of cars for the 1930 season, some changes to the Midget were introduced.

(Below) A ramp under the front half of the pneumatic seat cushion improves comfort. Newspapers folded as shown can be used experimentally to find the best height.

(Left) Celluloid side windows can be let into the hood at a small cost and bring about a great and very useful increase in driving visibility.

(Right) The inside of the tail, showing the spare oil and petrol tins, the tools strapped to the floor, and the side-screen bag at the back of the seat.

POINTS OF INTEREST. — A group of detail photographs of the car, showing the external Trico screenwiper, the tonneau cover in its two positions, the Stadium fog and road light and the instrument board; on the last named, the switch for the fog lamp and the valve for the wiper can just be seen to the left and right respectively of the steering-wheel boss.

Pictures published in a magazine article giving details of useful modifications made to the M-type. With the hood up taller people benefitted from the extra glazed areas in the roof.

Drawings by Connolly began to be used in MG catalogues and adverts.

Prior to building coupés for sale a number of different designs were tried before the Carbodies version was selected.

As the new premises were now a few miles away, it was no longer practical to use chassis from the Morris plant at Cowley. Anyway, the majority of components were actually manufactured in the Midlands and it was sensible for these to go directly from there to Abingdon. As the M-type was now to be built from scratch, some alterations could be made to the design of the Minor rolling chassis and running gear to make these more suited to a sporting car. The Morris rod and cable brakes and transmission handbrake were replaced by what was to become the standard MG system of Bowden cables operating from a cross-shaft in conjunction with the handbrake. This gave four-wheel braking on the handbrake and remained in use on all the MG models up to the introduction of hydraulic brakes for the T-series in 1936.

It is, perhaps, the change to the brakes that is the most noticeable difference between the early and later cars, with the Morris system fitted to the former having the front brake mechanism protruding through the louvres in the side panels.

About the time of the chassis changes the body design was altered and the subsequent units received from Carbodies, in crates of three, featured doors hinged on the forward edge instead of the rear, and with more substantial door rubbers introduced to prevent the doors rattling. Another change saw a modified way of adjusting the driver's seat, allowing a variable position of the seat cushion and rake of the squab. From open M-type number 2M 2260, engine number 2031A, the improved valve timing developed at Abingdon was used for the camshafts, increasing the

The later M-types had the doors hinged at the front.

Taken for distribution to the press or for publicity purposes, this is a good image to show the limited space available for the rear seat passengers.

A good selling point for the MG coachwork was the sunroof. Important also were the four small windows as they let extra light into what otherwise could have been a very enclosed space, especially for anyone squeezed into the back.

One of the first coupés was taken to a village near the factory for photography.

There was good access to the front seats.

power to 27bhp. Irrespective of their build date, most cars restored in recent years will have the improved power output.

To take full advantage of their increased production facilities MG needed to sell as many cars as they could. More imaginative marketing included giving Harold Connolly the task of drawing attractive pictures to illustrate sales brochures and magazine advertisements. His efforts for the 1930 brochure included a beautiful drawing of a blue M-type two-seater that was obviously about to take part in some sort of sporting event.

Introduced to the public for the first time at the 1929 London Motor Show, the Midget Sportsman's Coupé was an attempt to widen the market for the small MG by catering for those people who preferred closed cars. The coupé was described at the time as an occasional four, but really was no more than a two-seater with a very tiny bench seat in the back. At £245 it was more costly than the open version, but one was getting a car that was faster and more exclusive than the equivalent current Morris or Austin. Production of the coupé Midget began in earnest in February 1930. The list of bodies made for The MG Car Company by Carbodies of Coventry shows that a pattern coupé body was produced at the end of July 1929, two further bodies in October, perhaps for the motor show, and then a further 250 in November, all fabric covered. Almost a year later a further 250 fabric bodies were ordered.

The 4-cylinder OHC engine inherited by the

Placing MGs in interesting locations for pictures was something often done. Here the nearby Abingdon Airfield was a probable location.

Midget from the Minor was mated to a Wolseley three-speed gearbox. The early Midgets had a transmission handbrake that was fitted to the rear of the gearbox around the output shaft using an extra lug at the bottom of the rear gearbox casing as support. The transmission brake unit was also attached at the top to the cover from which also emerged the long gear lever. The drive to the gearbox from the engine used a heavy flywheel, within which sat the simple 6.5-inch Borg and Beck clutch mechanism. This was adequate for the engines producing only 20bhp, but for the later M- and D-types a larger 7.25inch clutch was used. Once the cars were built at Abingdon and had the cable-operated brakes all

The well-equipped cockpit of a restored MG M-type Salonette.

With metal-skinned bodywork this M-type was posed for pictures in the factory.

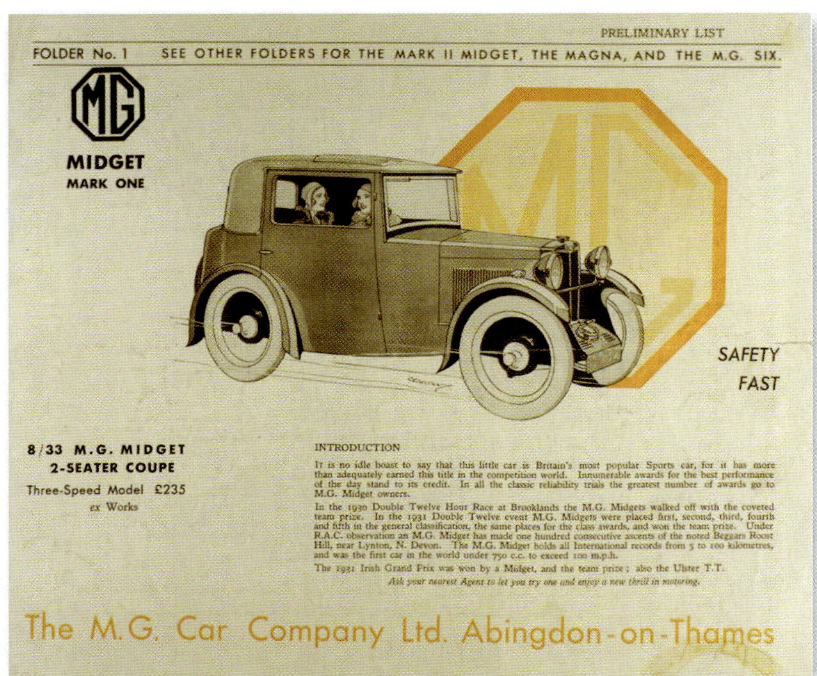

A preliminary brochure for the M-type Coupé.

Advertisement placed to persuade those going to the motor show to visit the MG stand to see the new Coupé.

Artwork for use in brochures and adverts.

A restored M-type with a metal-skinned body.

round the gearboxes no longer had the brackets for the transmission brake fitted.

Until the era of the T-type Midgets, the M-type was the most numerous of the pre-war MG models and its popularity amongst those interested in motor sport led to the formation in 1930 of a club exclusively for owners of MGs. It also led to increasing numbers of MG cars appearing in the entry lists for trials, rallies and club races.

The M-Type Midget In Motor Sport

From the outset, here was a car that just begged to be driven in competition by its largely youthful owners, and with deliveries of new Midgets to those enthusiastic drivers continuing throughout 1929 they began to enter events at club meetings in increasing numbers. In the early 1930s production car trials were the main and easily accessible branch of motor sport. The only proper motor racing circuit at that time was Brooklands, with other speed events being timed hillclimbing at venues like Shelsley Walsh and racing on improvised tracks, one example being Southport Sands. Many clubs held trials, but the most prestigious were those organised by the MCC that featured both motorcycles and cars. Of these three the one that attracted the most attention was the Land's End Trial. The 1929 trial attracted a large entry, but there is no doubt that the sight of the new MG Midgets, production of which had barely started at the Oxford factory, made an impression on reporters; one said of their ascent of Porlock, 'A great deal of interest naturally centred round the entry of four MG Midgets, and it would be difficult to imagine a more impressive display than they gave. Most ascents were faultless, with the drivers of the Midgets earning two gold and two silver awards.'

The 1930 Land's End Trial saw an increase in the number of competitors using MG Midgets. The trial that year started from the premises of The Slough Trading Estate and the route used two new hills, Grabhurst and Ruses Mill, in addition to established favourites Porlock, Lynmouth, Beggars' Roost and Bluehills Mine. There were no less than 31 Midgets, seven 18/80s and two of the earlier MGs in the event and the drivers amassed a total of 22 gold medals. MG was certainly starting to make a name on the motor sport scene.

We tend now to think of MGs only being exported worldwide from the late 1940s, but actually quite a number of the earlier models went abroad and a green M-type was exhibited at the New York Motor Show in 1930. MGs began to go to customers in many overseas countries and some were used there in motor sport of many types. The Monte Carlo rally was then considered the premier such event, attracting coverage in the major British motoring magazines and even the national press. These naturally tended to concentrate on entries from the home countries, of which there were increasing numbers during the 1930s. The first to feature an MG was the 1929 rally, when Sir Francis Samuelson entered an 18/80 Salonette. Some MGs had taken part in smaller events, like the Southport Rally, but none in the long-distance marathons

That first MG entry was fraught with difficulty. The weather was bad, posing problems for all entrants who chose Northern European staring points, including those from Britain. Sir Francis had his relief driver pull out at the last minute, meaning he drove throughout single-handed and on one occasion for 32 hours on end. He managed to do the trip in the scheduled time and was the only entry to do so without a change of driver. In the Mont des Mules hillclimb that followed the rally he made third fastest time of the day.'

Despite the problems in 1929, Samuelson entered again the following year, this time in an 18/80 Mark II. The 1930 event was the ninth Monte Carlo Rally to be run and that year the weather conditions were more favourable, although the 25 who began the journey from John-o-Groats had icier roads than those who chose other European starting points. There were two MGs in the rally, the second being the Land's End starting M-type Midget driven by F.M. Montgomery. Both cars were classified as finishers.

Traditionally the Monte Carlo Rally has never been over when the cars reach the principality. In 1930 the drivers were faced with tackling the Concours de Regularité, which comprised two circuits of a 50-mile mountain route and included some special tests. There was also a Concours de Confort where gold medals were on offer for those whose cars were judged to have the best coachwork and accessories. This competition did not, however, affect the overall results. In the hillclimb that year the 850cc Midget took first place in the 750cc–1100cc class.

The Monte Carlo M-type at Abingdon prior to the rally.

The hard-driven M-type in Monte Carlo at the end of the rally.

In 1931 there were MGs amongst the British entries in the Monte Carlo Rally. Starting from John-o-Groats, Francis Samuelson entered again, this time in a Midget Sportsman's Coupé, and Montgomery in an open Midget. There was also an entry from Norman Black in an 18/80 Speed Model. Additionally, a Portuguese-entered Midget started from Lisbon. Those setting out from Scotland had to contend with blizzards and icy roads, Black in the 18/80 having the additional problem of windscreen wipers that failed to wipe. British cars dominated the event and the overall winner was Donald Healey in his Invicta. Norman Black won a trophy and also was placed second in class in the hillclimb. The Midgets of Samuelson and Montgomery were well placed in the concours and Samuelson took the originality prize. The Lisbon M-type was also classified as a finisher, although lower down the order than the British-entered MGs.

The first outing for the Midgets on the track came with the Junior Car Club event at Brooklands in July 1929, where the drivers of three of the five Midgets entered achieved gold medals. Brooklands also staged another notable M-type competition success. Kimber had been approached by two enthusiastic Midget owners who felt that the cars, given some modification, were capable of winning the team prize in the 1930 Double Twelve-hour race at Brooklands. Based on the formula established by the successful twenty-four hour race at Le Mans, the British equivalent was run in two twelve-hour stints on the Friday and Saturday, so as not to spoil the beauty sleep of the affluent residents of

The 1929 Light Car Club High Speed Trial at Brooklands was the first race meeting on that circuit to see the new Midgets.

Five M-types entered in the 1930 Double-Twelve race lined up at the factory.

nearby St. George's Hill.

Modifications to the cars consisted of improving the power output of the 850cc engines by raising the compression ratio, polishing the cylinder heads and fitting a camshaft with improved valve timing. Additionally, the bodies were modified by giving them cut-down doors, an undershield to reduce drag, and staggered bucket seats for driver and riding mechanic. Also larger fuel tanks were specified, the headlamps were re-positioned closer to the radiator, the exhaust systems were modified and fold-down gauze racing windscreens replaced the standard V-screen. In a race marred by a fatal accident involving the Talbot team, the Midgets driven by Randall and Montgomery, Townend and Jackson, and Roberts and Pollard took the Team Prize.

Although outright victory at Le Mans has always been the preserve of the larger-capacity sports cars and out-and-out sports racing machinery, MGs competed there as early as 1930, when a couple of M-type Midgets were privately entered. The cars were specially prepared by the factory and fitted with modified bodies that had a flared scuttle very like the one seen on the prototype M-types displayed at the 1928 motor show. The pointed tail housed an18-gallon fuel tank in place of the standard 4.5-gallon scuttle-mounted unit. The spare wheel was moved from the tail to the nearside of the car and staggered seats were fitted. The usual M-type V-shaped windscreen was replaced with a full-width one. To run the pits the very experienced factory engineer 'Jacko' Jackson went to Le Mans.

Francis Samuelson and Freddie Kindell drove one car and the other was in the hands of R.C. Murton-Neale and Jack Hicks. The race started at 4pm on the Saturday afternoon and by just after nine that evening the Samuelson car was out with bearing failure. The cause has been given as the fracture of an oil pipe from the larger-capacity pump fitted. The second M-type fared little better. Murton-Neale had a contretemps with the fencing on one of the corners after skidding on sand placed by locals to stop such incidents occurring. So incensed was he by this that he reportedly flung the remains of the fencing at the troops guarding that part of the course. The car was eventually taken out of the running when the crankshaft broke. Initially this was thought to be caused by a foreign body blocking an oil-way. In their report of the race *The Motor* said that a piece of tape had been discovered blocking the oil filter and that this had mysteriously found its way from a plug lead into the lubrication system. The suggestion was that the car had been tampered with whilst being used on local journeys and that the team would have been wiser to leave the car in the paddock with the other racing cars. However, it was later found to be as a result of damage sustained in the accident fracturing a new oil pipe.

As soon as the race was over Captain Samuelson decided that he would like to enter the Belgian 24-hour Grand Prix two weeks later. With his engine now damaged and not repairable locally, he and co-driver Kindell decided to lift the engine out of the car and take it back in their support vehicle to Abingdon. Having telegraphed their intentions ahead, and in the expectation that engineer Jackson would also have returned, the drivers arrived at the factory and work started immediately on repairing and tuning the damaged engine. It took barely 24 hours for the

Two of the three cars that took the team award during the race.

A stunt involving 100 consecutive ascents of the difficult Beggar's Roost trials hill by a standard M-type was welcomed by the MG Car Company and used in advertisements.

The M-type ascending Beggar's Roost on one of the 100 runs.

work to be completed and the drivers managed to catch the ferry back to France on the Thursday and fit the engine to the car over the weekend. They left Le Mans in the M-type on the Monday evening for the 48-hour drive to the Spa circuit, so as to be ready for practice on the Thursday.

Running in the 1100cc class that comprised twelve cars, the Midget had the smallest engine capacity of them all. The Spa circuit at that time was over nine miles long and in some parts not well surfaced. Practice for the MG crew consisted of learning the circuit and how to cope with the steep camber on a few sections. As part of the race would be run in the dark, and many of the cars in the other classes would be considerably faster than their MG, they needed to be able to judge where it was safe to be off the racing line. Running steadily in the race, the Midget was at one time third in class and looked likely to be able to improve on this when misfortune saw the clutch start to slip. A quick visit to the pits for a squirt of fire extinguisher into the clutch housing produced a temporary cure, but further visits for repeat doses

Three of the LCC High Speed Trial M-types photographed at Abingdon.

were necessary and the MG began to drop down the order. In the end they finished fifth in class, still a creditable effort by these enthusiastic amateurs.

Good publicity was an important way to promote sales and the column inches in the general and motoring press devoted to the MG record-breaking, endurance runs and other feats were always welcome. So when in May 1930 Midget owner and trials enthusiast Kenneth Marsh suggested trying to make 100 consecutive ascents of the difficult Beggars' Roost hill near Lynton in Devon this was accepted and supported by the MG Car Company. Under the supervision of the RAC, Marsh succeeded in making the target in seven hours and during this time the engine was kept running whilst petrol and oil levels were topped up. The publicity machine ensured that the event received appropriate coverage in advertisements.

Another record attempt began in August 1930 when Captain Max Hay DFC and W.E. Wolveridge left the Royal Automobile Club in a newly registered M-type to try to circle the world in just five months. Aside from the initial reports in magazines, there seem to be no other references to the endeavour so we do not know if they succeeded. By the time their car was built all Midgets benefited from the improved power that came from fitting camshafts with the valve timing developed for the Double-Twelve cars and the replicas. Nevertheless, some owners craved even more horsepower and a popular way to achieve this was by supercharging.

The work carried out during 1931 on improving power output of the 750cc engines in the C-type Montlhéry Midgets resulted in the MG Car Company briefly offering a few of the final M-types fitted with a supercharger. A report early in 1932 on one of these in *The Autocar* gave the price as £250, an increase of £65 over the £185 charged then for the standard metal panelled car. By that time the last of those with fabric-covered bodies had been reduced to £165. No mention was made in the article as to whether the cars carried the usual guarantee as previous correspondence with owners who wished to fit a supercharger themselves had been told that this would invalidate the warranty.

The testers liked the performance, and particularly the extra torque from the supercharged engine that allowed better acceleration from lower engine speeds than with the un-supercharged car. This was particularly useful as the car tested had the three-speed gearbox with a large gap between ratios. Looking at the few figures they published, the top speed timed over a quarter-mile rose from the 63mph quoted in their 1930 test of a standard car to 75.63mph supercharged. Acceleration

One of the 12/12 M-types photographed in the factory.

Seen here during a trial is an M-type modified to Double-Twelve specification.

from 10mph to 30mph in second gear fell from 7.5 secs to 5.75secs and in top by over 4secs. In addition to the normal instruments there was a supercharger pressure gauge and the test car also had a push-pull control to dip the headlamps. The only downside was the need to add some oil to the fuel to lubricate the supercharger, but it was said that a metering device to introduce the oil was being developed to overcome this.

The M-Type 12/12 Replicas

Following the success of the team of M-type Midgets, in a manner that has since become a familiar marketing tool, replicas of the 'Double-Twelve' cars were catalogued for sale to the general public at £245 and in all 21 examples were built. Of these 18 chassis numbers are known to be 1986 to 1990 and from 2261 to 2273. A special brochure issued to promote sales of these cars described them as the 8/45 MG Midget Sports Double Twelve model.

Soon after the race the car driven at Brooklands by Randall was lent by University Motors to *Motor Sport* magazine for a test run. Despite having had no attention since the race, the car ran perfectly during a 200-mile drive to the West Country and the journalists reported that with the mildly tuned engine the car was capable of effortless cruising at 60mph and a maximum of over 70mph. A few weeks later, and after the availability of replicas to the public had been announced, the magazine had a further opportunity to test a car. They mentioned in their report that the engines of these Double Twelve cars were specially assembled with a modified camshaft, stronger valve springs, special inlet and exhaust manifolds and a different SU carburettor. The engines were all run in and checked before delivery to the customer. The body featured cut-down tops to the doors and the cars had a larger fuel tank and full-width windscreen with either gauze mesh or Triplex glass fitted. For owners intent on serious competition work all the nuts and bolts could be wired or split-pinned and an undershield could be fitted, this work was at extra cost. The dashboard carried an oil temperature gauge and a water thermometer in addition to the standard oil pressure, speedometer and ammeter instruments.

An Epic of . .

The Double-Twelve

being the story of twenty-four hours of consistent running at high speed by five M.G. Midgets and the winning of the coveted Team Prize

Miss Victoria Worsley and the M.G. Midget she drove in The Double-Twelve-Hour Race.

ISSUED BY THE PUBLICITY DEPARTMENT OF THE M.G. CAR COMPANY LIMITED, ABINGDON-ON-THAMES

One of the catalogues issued to help sell the Double-12 replicas.

This M-type appears to have been one of the 12/12 replicas.

Special Bodied M-Types

A total of 3235 M-type Midgets were built and sold; of these over 500 were Coupés and 82 left the factory as rolling chassis for completion by outside coachbuilders. Jarvis of Wimbledon were the most prolific suppliers of special-bodied versions. When the MG Car Company moved from Oxford to Abingdon in late 1929 they began building the Midget rolling chassis there rather than modifying ones collected from the Morris Cowley works. Improvements were also incorporated and for the first time the Midget rolling chassis was made available without bodywork. This presented Jarvis of Wimbledon with the opportunity to build and sell a much-improved version in time for the 1930 Olympia Motor Show. Pictures and details of the new model appeared in the press prior to the event. Priced initially at £215, but raised a month later to £225, it was offered as being available in three different colour schemes. The MG Car Company approved the Jarvis Midget to meet a demand for a de luxe body. The specification included leather upholstery for the bucket seats, a three-piece windscreen and a better hood that could be easily raised and lowered.

A full road test on the Jarvis Midget was published in *Motor Sport* magazine in January 1931. After praising the soundness of the design of the Midget chassis, allied to successes in competition, the magazine went on to say that the Jarvis body was both good looking and practical. In their opinion that version of the Midget provided comfort, plus the ability to stow a reasonable amount of baggage behind the seats for touring. In the floor of the rear compartment one hatch gave access to the rear axle for maintenance, while a second led to the dummy rear fuel tank that served as a toolbox. Like the standard model, the petrol was carried in a tank at the back of the engine compartment.

The twin bucket seats were adjustable, although on

Advertisement placed by Jarvis of Wimbledon features the earlier models with the external surface of the bodywork covered with fabric rather than metal.

Later Jarvis M-type with metal covering the wooden frame of the special body.

Two of the Jarvis M-types.

the test car they would not accommodate those over six feet tall, something remedied on later cars. The hood fabric was permanently attached to the rear of the body so raising the hood and frame was a one-man operation. When lowered, a cover was provided to both conceal the lowered hood and provide protection for the rear compartment. Like the standard M-type, the wooden-framed body of the Jarvis was covered in coloured fabric on the earlier cars and only metal-panelled on later models.

The *Motor Sport* test team commented very favourably on the ride and roadholding, saying that it felt as good as much larger sports cars. The steering, however, was thought to be too light and low-geared and the handbrake lever placed further forward than was convenient. The top speed recorded was 68mph, with 40mph being the optimum point to change up from second to top on the three-speed box. The OHC power unit was said to be the smooth and free revving, producing a good power output for so small a capacity and capable of accelerating from walking pace to maximum speed in top gear. This was a desirable feature before the arrival of synchromesh gears. The model proved popular and although the exact number of Jarvis Midgets built is not recorded, it is likely that a fair number of those sold as rolling chassis went there.

Information about other coachbuilders taking Midgets is incomplete. However it is known that the University Motors drophead coupé foursome with wind-up windows in high-sided doors was built for them by Carlton. M.A. McEvoy of Notting Hill Gate offered four-seater conversions of the standard M-type body at a cost of £25; this price included a full windscreen. The same company also fitted their body to at least one new MG chassis. Jensen Motors of West Bromwich also bodied at least one chassis, and Hoyle Bodybuilding Corporation (1928) Limited, well known for their bus bodies, in the final stages before the company ceased trading in August 1931, built a foursome DHC on an M-type chassis.

This Jarvis M-type is regularly seen at MG Car Club events.

An odd one this, an M-type chassis fitted with van bodywork. Built for some local deliveries and collections, it was also used for publicity on record attempts.

One odd M-type was the so-called High Speed Van. This was built using the chassis and other parts recovered from an M-type that had been written off by the insurance company after the owner had crashed it while driving in France. Presumably the factory used the van to carry out some local collection and delivery duties, but it was also a useful publicity tool at the record-breaking attempts on Pendine Sands by EX127. In more recent years a replica was built and occasionally exhibited.

Although the original van did not survive, this modern replica has appeared at some events.

SPECIFICATION M-TYPE

Wheelbase/track	6' 6"/3' 6"	
Suspension	Leaf springs front and back	
Wheels/tyres	Wire, centre laced, bolt on 2.50" x 19"/4.00"x19"	
Brake drum size	8 inch	
Engine/power output	847cc/20bhp	
	Later cars and 12/12 replicas 27bhp	
Build dates	13th April 1929 to 1st June 1932	
12/12 Replicas	30th April 1930 to 1st December 1930	
Cars built	2-seater fabric body	2329
	2-seater metal panelled	273
	Coupé fabric body	493
	Coupé metal panelled	37
	12/12 replicas	21
	Rolling chassis	82
	Total	**3235**

The C-Type Montlhery Midget

Of all the many four-cylinder MG Midgets built between 1929 and 1955 it is the C-type Montlhéry Midget that had the greatest number of successes on the track and was probably the model most responsible for establishing the enduring sporting reputation of the marque. It was not the first to be offered by the factory in ready-to-race trim, that honour went to the Double-Twelve M-types and the 18/100 Tigress. However, it was the first to give its owners a car running in the 750cc class capable of giving a good account of itself in a wide variety of events.

The M-Type had proved a sales success, but its potential for further development as a sports car was severely limited by the Morris Minor chassis with its short wheelbase and high centre of gravity. It had been realised that another chassis was really required if the Midget was to be developed for road and track, and an entirely new ladder-frame chassis had already been designed. This had the two main chassis members set parallel to each other and passing under the rear axle to keep them as low as possible. The side members were united by cross tubes brazed into cast and turned mounting brackets and riveted in place. Each of the leaf road springs was pivoted at the front but held at the rear by bronze trunnions, rather than by conventional shackles. The radiator was fixed to an extension of the front engine support and the entire power unit, gearbox and radiator were carried on a three-point mounting to isolate them from chassis flexing. Eight-inch brake drums were used, with cable operation from a cross-shaft. The driver could adjust the handbrake operating on all four wheels by turning a wing nut adjacent to the brake lever.

As described in another section, the first appearance of the new chassis was in the record breaker EX120. This car, fitted with a highly modified version of the M-type power unit with the capacity reduced to 743cc, became the first 750cc car to travel

One of the first cars completed was photographed prior to the Double-Twelve-Hour Race.

Photographed with what may have been C0254 is the Hon. Mrs Chetwynd, who purchased C0260 and raced the car in the Double-Twelve-Hour Race and in other events, including at Le Mans.

100 miles in an hour. The attempt took place at the Paris Montlhéry track and attracted a goodly amount of attention for MG. In the wake of this Kimber announced that a new 750cc sports/racing car was to be made available to the public, called the MG Midget Mk ll Montlhéry Model.

The Light Car issue for 6th March 1931 carried a description of the Mark II Midget, or C-type, and gave ready-to-race prices of £295 without a supercharger and £345 fitted with a Powerplus blower. The car was described as being suitable for touring, but also to race at Brooklands or elsewhere. The engine was outwardly similar to that used in the M-type, but had a crankshaft with stroke reduced by 10mm, giving a capacity of 746cc. The crankshaft was further described as being stiffer, with larger big end bearings and a more substantial rear main bearing than the one used for the M-type. Shorter pistons with reinforced crowns were used to cope with the higher compression ratio and also with supercharging. A cast sump with adequate exterior fins helped cool the oil, the level being maintained through a float in the sump fed by a reserve oil tank on the firewall. Drive to the rear axle was through a four-speed ENV gearbox with a cross-tube rear mounting and intermediate gear ratios of 4.02:1, 2.0:1 and 1.36:1. A close-ratio alternative had higher first and second gears of 2.69:1 and 1.86:1.

The rear fuel tank either used a hand-operated pump to pressurise the tank and push fuel to the carburettor or supercharger or had an electric pump. At first the inlet and exhaust ports were on the same side of the cylinder head and the engine produced 37.4bhp without a supercharger and 44.9bhp in blown form. Later the cross-flow head with inlet and exhaust on

C0261 was purchased new by H.C. Hamilton of University Motors and entered by him in the Double-Twelve-Hour Race without a supercharger, finishing third. After the race a supercharger was fitted and then Hamilton entered his car in the German Grand Prix at the very demanding Nürburgring circuit, finishing first in the 800cc class.

One of the C-types that ran initially un-supercharged in the Double-Twelve-Hour Race and was later fitted with a blower driven off the front of the crankshaft. The M-type van is in the background.

opposite sides boosted power to 44.1bhp without a blower and 52.5bhp supercharged. The pretty pointed-tail body fitted to the C-type Midget was of ash-framed construction and the tail section concealed the spare wheel, much as had been the case with the M-type. An attractive feature of the body was the twin-humped scuttle sitting above a workmanlike instrument panel. This followed racing car practice of the time and for many years remained a prominent part of the design of MG sports car bodies.

In its 20th November 1931 issue *The Autocar* published a road test of a supercharged C-type Midget and this provides a contemporary record of what you had for an outlay of £575, about three times the price of the last M-type two-seater sports models. The road testers pointed out that the price reflected the amount of care taken building each car individually. If used for road trips the article said that the 15-gallon fuel tank would, at 27mpg, give a safe range of around 350 miles. In a race the car would use more fuel and after rather less miles had been covered would need to visit the pits to refuel during longer events. To speed up these stops, quick release caps were provided for the tank and also the radiator. Easy adjustment of brakes and shock absorbers was provided. Fuel and ignition supply systems were duplicated.

After the cars entering the initial race meetings had been completed, an assembly line was set up to build the remaining cars for sale to customers.

On the road a test car that had already been used in two gruelling events and had been driven many road miles, top speed was about 88mph and acceleration brisk as long as the engine speed was kept over 2500rpm. Normal maximum rpm was 5500, probably exceeded on track. A low first gear made using the car to ascend trials hills practical. Superb roadholding and brakes were featured, as was the comprehensive range of instruments and switches on the dashboard. Comfortable bucket seats were mentioned, while a hood and supports could be stored in the tail alongside the spare wheel. Space for baggage was provided behind the seats and in the tail.

Of the 44 cars built quite a number survive and others are probably still around awaiting discovery. In addition, the availability of early D-type chassis of a similar size and construction has led to some of these being restored to resemble C-types.

The C-Type In Motor Sport

With his eye firmly fixed on the publicity to be gained by dominating the 750cc class, Kimber decided that the first outing for the initial batch of cars to leave the factory was to be the 1931 Double-Twelve race at Brooklands, due to be staged just two months after the decision to build the cars had been taken. This seems an impossibly short time to complete the cars and the Abingdon staff had to work at full stretch to get ready for the event.

The Junior Car Club Double-Twelve was the British equivalent of the famous annual Le Mans event. Unlike in France, the use of public roads for racing was banned in England so it had to be run at Brooklands, which was the only suitable available venue. Unfortunately that track is situated close to St. George's Hill, Weybridge, which was, and still remains, a very exclusive private estate occupied by many influential people. Noisy cars circulating the nearby track tended to upset the peace and tranquillity they felt they had the right to expect. In consequence cars could not have open exhausts, hence the Brooklands silencer, and certainly were not be allowed to carry on through the night. To get round this, the race was divided into two 12-hour stints, the cars being locked away overnight so that while the race was not in progress no repairs or servicing were permitted.

As with nearly every race run in England at the time, a handicap system was employed for the Double-Twelve. This consisted of minimum race distances to be covered to qualify and these varied from class to class. The trick here was to beat the handicapper as well as other competitors, and for their first outing the new Midgets now ran in the 750cc class at something of an advantage as there were no earlier performances as a guide. The previous year the M-types were not up against Austin Sevens in the 750cc category, the 847cc MGs entered ran in the up to 1100cc class where the best they could achieve against the 1089cc Rileys was to take the team prize. The C-types in 1931 ran un-supercharged and thus had an advantage over the factory-entered supercharged Austins, which were expected to circulate some 30 per cent faster than the un-supercharged cars. This was too much to expect and, although the Austins were actually able to lap quicker than the 1100cc cars in the class above them, they could not beat their handicap over the MGs and thus took no awards.

It was an all-out effort for those involved with preparing the cars for the race as there were no less than 14 C-types entered and all were immaculately turned out, despite the whole batch being assembled in two weeks from newly-produced parts. All the cars were delivered to Brooklands in time for their drivers to take part in the first practice session. One of the cars entered by the Earl of March ran a bearing in practice and the engine was immediately changed. Cecil Kimber himself had the job of running it in by driving overnight on public roads. For spectators the 1931 race held less interest than it might have because drivers of cars with larger-capacity engines realised they had no chance of an award as the handicapping system in use favoured those with smaller engines, so many decided not to enter. However, for the drivers and mechanics 24 hours of high-speed running on the rough concrete track was anything but a picnic. The race was for production sports cars and as such they were required to carry full road equipment, lights, wings, etc. As the race progressed the buffeting caused many of these components to work loose and time was lost in the pits for repairs.

Motor racing in the early years of the last century was very much the preserve of rich and well-connected members of society, and by 1931 Brooklands could almost be regarded as much a part of the social season as Henley or Ascot. Those able to afford to buy the new Midgets to race them at Brooklands were unlikely to be wage earners from the same social class as those who built the cars. The majority were young men and women from privileged backgrounds and well used to having wealth,

C0263 was the factory demonstrator and driven in the Double-Twelve-Hour Race by H.H. Sistead and F.R. Kindell, but retired with mechanical problems. Now supercharged, it did a demonstration run at Shelsley Walsh and was entered in the Ulster Tourist Trophy and 500-mile Race at Brooklands. First car to have a cross-flow cylinder head and close-ratio ENV gearbox, it was lent to the press for road testing.

C0257 finished the Double-Twelve-Hour Race second overall before being supercharged to run at the Nürburgring, where it was so badly damaged as to need a complete rebuild. It. Was fitted with a new chassis and a single-seat body.

C0278 was sold as a rolling chassis to be fitted with a Jarvis body.

property and servants. Many had met each other whilst at university, or at schools like Eton. The Earl of March was, of course, not just the heir to the Goodwood estate and the future ninth Duke of Richmond and Gordon, but also a tremendous enthusiast of things mechanical, especially racing cars. Another one of the owners was the Honourable Mrs Joan Chetwynd. She had married 23-year-old Adam Duncan Chetwynd in 1928 and they lived at 30 East St. Helens Street in Abingdon, very near the factory. In 1929 she had taken the class F 12-hour record at Brooklands driving a Lea Francis, a marque also raced by her husband. Chetwynd-Talbot was the family name of the Earl of Shrewsbury and Waterford so when she ordered her C-type she had it finished in the Talbot family horse-racing colours of silver and red.

The MGs suffered their share of problems. Early on an 850cc M-type had engine failure, the Stisted/Kindell C-type had broken its clutch, and Joan Chetwynd's car was in the pits for a time with ignition problems. A number of engines suffered valve spring failure, attributed by the factory to a fault in manufacture, but some were repaired and returned to the race. By the time the first 12-hour stint was over four of the brand new Midgets were out of the race permanently and many others were looking distinctly second hand.

The next day, when the starting signal was given (it was a Saturday as they did not race on Sundays), not a car left the line, as this was the time that the mechanics could start refuelling and repairing entries they had not been able to touch overnight. Once the cars were back

C0272 was sold by MG dealer Knott Bros Limited of Bournemouth to George A. Thomas as a road car fitted with appropriate extras. George entered a number of club events, including the MCC High-Speed Trial at Brooklands and Land's End Trial.

on the track it became clear that the Midgets in the lead, those of the Earl of March's team, had slowed slightly to preserve their engines. Joan Chetwynd's car had been one of those to suffer valve spring trouble and an hour was lost fitting a new spring before she could start the second day's racing. A few laps later Ron Horton's red-painted Midget expired and was pushed off the track, followed soon after by the Chetwynd car, which had finally given up the struggle.

When the flag fell at the end of the second day the result was a triumph for MG. Half of the 14 C-types entered were still running and Midgets were in first, second, third, fourth and fifth places overall. The car driven by the Earl of March with C.S. Staniland was placed first and his three green-painted cars took the team prize. A large proportion of the Abingdon work force had travelled to Surrey to cheer for their entries and so the people who had toiled to finish the cars in time for the race witnessed the victory.

There was little time for celebration, however, as 11 of the Midgets were entered in the Irish Grand Prix held in Phoenix Park Dublin on 5/6th June, four weeks after the Brooklands event. Once again the cars ran with road equipment and the MGs were still un-supercharged. The smaller-capacity classes competed on the first day and the larger the second, with the results overall being decided by a handicap system. Again the MGs were favoured by the handicappers and had to maintain an average speed of 62.4mph. The supercharged 750cc Austins had a target of 69.4mph and those in the larger-capacity classes had an even-higher target. The race was run in appalling weather, which favoured the slower cars, and by the end the leading Midget had exceeded its target speed by 2.36mph, the first Austin by just over one fifth of a mile per hour and the best Riley by 1.49mph. Thus the MG driven by Norman Black won the event, with the three MGs entered by Goldie Gardner taking the team prize.

Mrs Chetwynd entered her car for the 1000 Mile Race at Brooklands on 3/4th June 1931, this time driven by Adam Chetwynd and Miss Veronica Worsley. Unfortunately the engine failed again. A connecting-rod went through the side of the block, so it was back to Abingdon for repair and preparation for the next major event, the 1931 24-hour race at Le Mans on June 13/14th June where there were two MGs entered. Both were C-types, one was driven by Samuelson and Kindell, the other by the Hon. Mrs Chetwynd and Stisted. Records show that when the Chetwynd car was at the factory it was fitted with items like bonnet straps, extra lamps and fittings to carry spare plugs, bulbs, etc. The factory also supplied a quantity of spares on loan. Both cars were running un-supercharged.

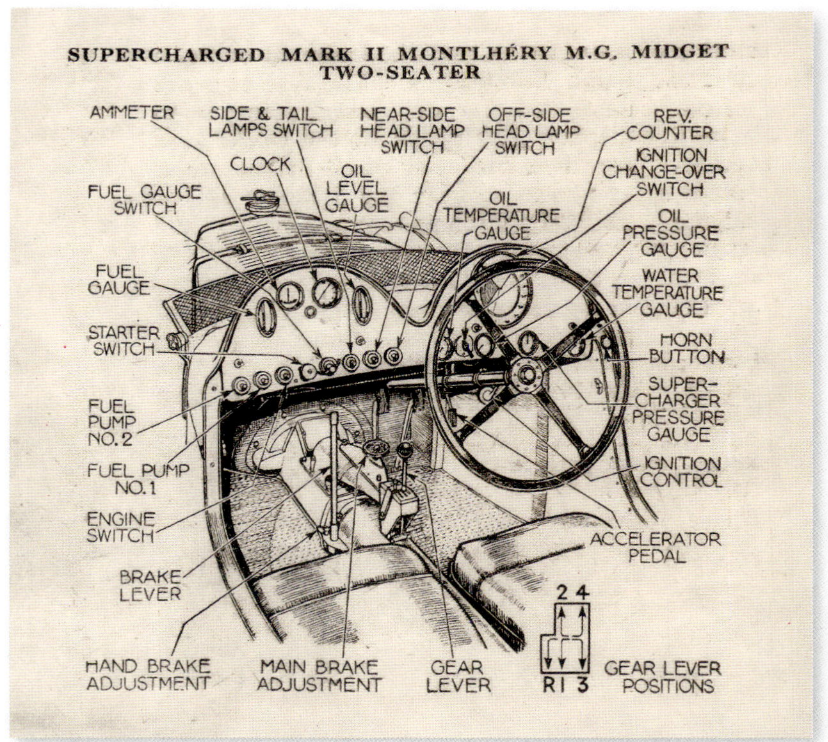

Detail drawings of the dashboard and shock absorber published in The Autocar *article describing the C-type.*

Neither car featured in the final results. Mrs Chetwynd's car went out of the race when the engine stopped out on the circuit. This was first diagnosed as a sheared key, later found to be a seized rocker shaft, and had the car failed near the pits then repairs would have been possible. The Samuelson car was involved in a collision with a bank after Kindell spun to avoid another competitor, and this caused delays for repairs to a broken rear spring mounting. A piston failed just before 3.30 pm on the Sunday, but the engine could still be persuaded to run. Samuelson left

the pits with, he thought, just under the half-an-hour permitted to complete the lap. Unfortunately the clock in the car was wrong and it was just over 30 minutes to the end of the race. Having driven slowly round the circuit he crossed the line at 4pm, having waited just short of the finish line for a few minutes. He was showered with congratulations, only to later be disqualified when it was discovered that the last lap took over the maximum permitted half-an-hour.

After the race the Chetwynd C-type was shipped home and collected from Southampton Docks by someone from the factory. It was repaired ready to take part in the Light Car Club Relay Race at Brooklands on 25th July. There it was involved in an accident and needed a considerable amount of work to the chassis. The car was used after this for a number of events, including the LCC Relay Race the following year. There it ran in a mixed team with two Rileys that took third place at an average speed of 84.92mph. By now preparation may have been in the hands of Brooklands-based Thomson and Taylor as they ordered some spares, including a new block, in June 1932. The car was evidently disposed of not too long afterwards, and was certainly in other hands by 1935, the year Mrs Chetwynd gave birth to a son and possibly ceased motor racing.

The other C-type Midgets had equally busy lives, often with more success. Thirteen were entered in the August Tourist Trophy Race held in Ulster, and all but two of the MGs, plus all bar one of the Austins, were running supercharged in what was a handicap event. Yet again, the MGs did well, with Norman Black winning overall, Stan Crabtree in third place and the cars taking first, second and third in class.

The Hon. Mrs Chetwynd with her C-type during the 1931 Double-Twelve at Brooklands. Her car failed to finish the race.

Two of the cars of the Randall team on track during practice for the Double-Twelve.

The factory was working on improving the power output of the engine and the first result of this was the arrival of the cross-flow cylinder head, which started appearing on the cars from mid-1932. As has been mentioned earlier, all the later C-type Midgets were fitted with conventional radiator grilles from new and the owners of most of the earlier cars had them converted to this specification, especially necessary for road racing or when the engines were supercharged and likely to run hotter.

The C-type continued to have success on road and track and most of the cars were developed progressively. Individual owners and tuning firms made changes to the cars without reference to the factory as they strove to gain an advantage over other cars or the handicapper. Ron Horton's car, for example, was fitted with special bodywork and used by him for record breaking, with some success. Tuning exponents like 'Wilkie' Wilkinson were able to extract far more out of these cars than had ever been envisaged by their designers, and even now C-types still give a good account of themselves in vintage events. They may not have the charisma and status of a K3, but they were still some of the most successful sports/racing cars of their time.

Specification C-Type

Wheelbase/track	6' 9"/3' 6"
Suspension	Leaf springs front and back
Wheels/tyres	Side-laced Rudge type 2.50" x 19"/4.00"x19"
Brake drum size	8 inch, later 12 inch
Engine/power output	746cc unsupercharged 37.4bhp to 44.1bhp
	Supercharged 44.9bhp to 52.5bhp
Gearbox	4-speed no synchromesh
Build dates	2nd May 1931 to 8th June 1932
Cars built	44 (C0728 sold as chassis and fitted with Jarvis coachwork)

Publicity booklet for the C-type.

Brochure describing the C-type.

The D-Type Midget

The D-type is often regarded as the poor relation of the OHC Midgets. Aimed when new at the family enthusiast and built in relatively small numbers, it has had less appeal as a restoration project than a J- or P-type two-seater sports model. However, largely due to the efforts of members of the MG D Group, there are now a reasonable number of D-types restored to original specification, rather than being rebuilt as replica C-types or other two-seater sports/racing cars. Because of the many similarities to the F-type Magna launched at the same time, restorers working on D-types have had a wider selection of parts and expertise available to them than might be expected for such a small production run.

The considerable effort needed to design and develop the C-type chassis would obviously not have been worthwhile for it to be used only in a small batch of competition cars. It thus would have come as no surprise to see a press announcement in September 1931 that versions of the C-type chassis were to be used for standard production cars. It was revealed that for the 1932 season there were to be open and closed four-seater models powered by either four-cylinder or six-cylinder engines and all would have versions of this chassis. The four-cylinder cars were described in catalogues as the 8/33 Midget (long chassis) to distinguish them from the earlier model based on the Morris Minor, now described in the same publication as just the 8/33 Midget. The new cars were just designated as D-types and were available alongside the two-seater M-type that remained on sale, the last examples leaving the production line as late as June 1932. The D-type was built on a three-inch longer version of the C-type chassis, but with the cross-tube mounting plates riveted, rather than bolted, to the

Factory picture of a D-type four-seat tourer.

The engine compartment of the prototype four-seat tourer.

D0382 has the later, longer chassis and this restored example shows the good weather protection provided with the hood and side-screens in place.

chassis side rails. The engine, transmission and brakes were taken straight out of the M-type, but the three-speed gearbox was fitted with a remote control. The one used for the D-type differed from the previous M-type arrangement attached directly to the top of the gearbox as it had a separate, shorter lever in a neat gate as part of the remote-control unit. Fairly soon after launch of the new model a four-speed gearbox was made available at an extra cost of £30. Unlike the M-type with its Morris Minor bolt-on wheels, the D-type chassis followed the C-type in having the Rudge-Whitworth type hubs with eared locking nuts. The spare wheel was mounted vertically at the back of the body.

All the first 100 cars built were equipped with an attractive open four-seater body. This had two front-hinged, cut-away doors and, unlike the M-type, the petrol tank, which still only held six gallons, was safely located in the rear of the chassis with fuel delivered to the engine by the earliest form of SU electric pump, the Petrolift. Another improvement was the upgrading of the car electrics from 6 to 12 volt. The cycle wings were of a similar design to those fitted to the last of the M-type two-seaters. Having a deeper section than those on the earlier Midgets and with the front ones provided with fairings between the wings and body sides, these gave improved protection from spray. The front bucket seats and the small pair of seats at the back were trimmed in leather, with a choice of green, brown, blue, red or grey finish. The coachwork as standard was black,

D0382 is a car with the later chassis and the longer doors that make accessing the rear seat easier.

D0311 is a correctly restored early D-type tourer with the shorter chassis.

Despite having the shorter chassis, D0311 still provides adequate room for the rear seat passengers.

The engine compartment of D0311.

with the wheels sprayed to match the chosen colour for the upholstery. At extra cost a range of two-tone colour schemes was on offer.

Experience with the first batch of cars showed the chassis to be too flexible, and after 100 D-types had been built the side rail section was strengthened and the wheelbase increased by two inches. The range of models was widened by the inclusion of a neat four-seater Salonette. Coachwork for this and the open car was to all intents and purposes identical to that fitted to the contemporary six-cylinder F-types. The closed coachwork fitted to the D-type was designed to appeal to those looking for a sporting saloon capable of transporting a couple of small children in the rear seats. Nice touches were the sliding sunshine roof with its inset glazed panels, an opening windscreen, arm rests for all occupants and a polished wooden dashboard.

As the engine with the timing improvements introduced during the life of the M-type produced just 27bhp, the extra weight of the body and chassis and, potentially, extra passengers, took the edge off any reasonable performance the car may have possessed. The manufacturers did offer a supercharger at an extra cost of £65, but those taking up the option were advised that the usual guarantee covering the engine was withdrawn 'as considerable damage can result by a lack of discretion on the part of the driver over which the Company has no control.'

It is unlikely many paid the considerable premium asked for a supercharger and later in life the D-type

D0464 is a later car restored to original condition with black paintwork and deep red colour trim and wheels.

The standard D-type instrument panel had only the gauge on the right for oil pressure. This showed white in all segments if pressure was high enough and red if too low. This has been supplemented here with a later gauge giving readings for oil pressure and water temperature.

developed a reputation for being underpowered. However, this may not be entirely fair as the performance can only be described as poor when compared to the later MG models. When the car was new few small four-seater cars would have enjoyed much more performance and most would have had less, so D-type owners were probably quite happy with the 45 to 50mph cruising speed of their purchase. The biggest disappointment would have been the retention of the M-type's three-speed gearbox, and those who either chose the four-speed option or fitted one later would have found the car to be much improved.

Although the M-type engine and gearbox were used for the D-type, there had been other improvements to the design not already mentioned. The main one was fitting a camshaft with altered valve timing that liberated more power, increasing the 20bhp from the early cars to 27bhp. All the small capacity OHC Midgets had oil pumps driven from the front of the crankshaft, but the designs varied. The first M-types had the an oil capacity of six pints in a pressed steel sump and an oil pump thought suitable for use in the Morris Minor. When power was first increased for the Double-Twelve cars a cast aluminium sump was designed to lower what had been increased to a gallon of oil into the flow of cooler air passing under the car. A revised oil pump capable of increased oil flow rate was fitted. The early D-types inherited a cast magnesium sump from the C-type but later cars had them made from aluminium alloy. The higher-capacity oil pump was also fitted.

Despite the appeal of the closed car, the majority of the D-type chassis were fitted with the open tourer body. On the last few of these the cut-away on the top

The later, longer chassis on D0464 does have more room to access the rear seat.

The engine compartment of a later tourer.

Tourer catalogue.

Salonette catalogue.

of the doors was altered from being straight across to dropping down towards the back, as became the norm on all the later OHC Midgets. Five D-types left the factory as rolling chassis. Two were fitted with Jarvis bodies, similar to those fitted by that company to the M-type and F-type, and three were given attractive 2/3-seater coachwork by the Baker Street, London, Alfa-Romeo dealer Stiles Limited.

Now overshadowed by the later and more celebrated OHC MGs, the D-type is still something of a rarity and as such may in future years attract greater interest and perhaps even a higher value.

Specification D-Type

Wheelbase/track	7' first 100 cars and 7' 2" later cars/3' 6"
Suspension	Leaf springs front and back
Wheels/tyres	Side-laced Rudge type 2.50" x 19"/4.00"x19"
Brake drum size	8 inch
Engine/power output	847cc/27bhp
Gearbox	3-speed no synchromesh
Build dates	9th October 1931 to 5th May 1932
Cars built	Tourers 208 Salonettes 37 Rolling chassis 5

EX120, The First MG Record Breaker

Initially it might be useful to explain the significance of the EX, or experimental, prefix. This was first used in 1928 when the prototype 18/80 models were being built and the factory designated the three prototype chassis as EX1, EX2 and EX3. The next number, EX4, was used when the Mark II 18/80 was developed and at that time it seems they had then intended to use just one number for all aspects of a new model. Following the move to Abingdon in 1929 a new register was started with the first number being 101, and an entry was to be given to each alteration to a current model or completely new car, with numbers EX101 to 119 allocated to changes to existing cars. EX120 was set aside for the new chassis MG was developing for the Midget, and that number remained on castings that hold the chassis cross tubes right up to T-type days. Because a prototype chassis was used for the first of the record breakers this was given the designation EX120.

George Eyston was technical director of the supercharger suppliers, Powerplus Limited, and a keen competitor and record breaker. His combined talents as a fearless competitor and gifted engineer were to make him one of the most successful members of that elite band of British speed record holders who received such an enormous amount of publicity in the 1930s. It was fortunate for the company that for the early years of that decade his name was often linked to MG. At Cambridge George had shared rooms with James Palmes, who ran Jarvis and Sons of Wimbledon. He wanted to raise the 750cc speed records using a modified Midget and George had the idea of using a reduced-capacity Riley engine for the same purpose. They decided to combine their efforts and went to see Cecil Kimber at Abingdon to discuss the project. There they discovered that the MG Car Company was working on a completely new chassis better suited to their task than a standard M-type.

One of a number of pictures taken in the MG factory of the chassis of an 1100cc French Rally two-seater. The Rally was possibly the inspiration behind the new MG chassis design.

Advertisement publicising the first records taken by EX120 without a supercharger.

As the ordinary M-type engine displacement was 847cc it was obviously necessary to bring the capacity down to no more than 750cc. Austin held these records with a supercharged car but the initial intention was to try to take them away with an unblown engine and then later raise the speed to over 100mph by fitting a supercharger. A special crankshaft reduced the stroke from 83 to 81mm and liners in the cylinder bores reduced these from 57 to 54mm and the capacity to 743cc. The rolling chassis with the modified engine was given a two-seater body. At Montlhéry on December 30th 1930 new records were set at speeds of around 87mph, about the limit unsupercharged.

At Montlhéry on February 16th 1931, after fitting a cowl to stop carburettor icing, Eyston set new records,

Running at Brooklands supercharged and with a cowl for the radiator, EX120 set more records.

EX120 photographed in the MG factory.

The fire damage on EX120 was so extensive that it was scrapped as being uneconomic to repair.

Records that no one can beat!

The record breaking M.G. Montlhéry Midget at speed with MR. G. E. T. EYSTON at the wheel

The first car in the world, of 750 cc., to exceed 100 m.p.h.— The first car in the world, of 750 cc., to cover over 100 miles in one hour, from a standing start.

One hundred and one miles in one hour were covered by Mr. J. A. Palmes' Montlhéry Midget driven by Mr. G. E. T. EYSTON, at the Montlhéry Track, on September 25th, 1931.

The car was fitted with a Powerplus Supercharger

The following International Class H records were secured: -

50 Kilometres 98. 7 m.p.h.
50 Miles - 99. 8 m.p.h.
100 Kilometres 100. 3 m.p.h.
100 Miles - 100.09 m.p.h.

1 hoyr 101 miles

MG publicity was designed to derive the maximum benefit from any sporting achievements. This advert heralds the first 750cc car to exceed 100mph, driven by George Eyston at Montlhéry.

EX120 on show at Abingdon alongside a C-type chassis.

all over 100mph. MG could claim to be the first 750cc car to exceed 100mph. This was the last time EX120 ran, as during a final slowing down lap it caught fire and George Eyston had to climb onto the tail of the car as he tried to stop it. He baled out before the car finally came to a halt. The car was never rebuilt, although the engine survives.

EX127 Record Breaker

With the fire-damaged EX120 not worth repairing a replacement was needed. Even prior to that last run Reg Jackson had already built an unfinished scale model at home of a possible new car, and Cecil Kimber authorised its completion in the factory. After testing the finished model in an aircraft wind tunnel, the overall design received approval from George Eyston and Kimber. To reduce wind resistance to the absolute minimum, in section the car was to be just big enough to accommodate Eyston seated as low down as possible. To achieve this the C-type chassis used was fitted with a specially built rear axle that placed the differential unit tight up against the left-hand rear wheel. Setting the engine, gearbox and prop shaft at a seven-degree angle allowed the driver to sit alongside the transmission, rather than above it. The car was so tightly tailored to Eyston's dimensions that he found it fairly difficult to drive; those of smaller stature, like Bert Denly, were more at home.

The car was taken to Montlhéry at the time of the last run of EX120 and tested by Ernest Eldridge after that car caught fire and George Eyston was injured. However, it was found that the very small air inlet for the radiator dictated by the supercharger installation caused the car to overheat badly. Any serious running was out of the question and the car went back to Abingdon. Initially the cure was thought to be a more efficient surface radiator, as used in many contemporary aircraft, but this proved unable to survive the battering it received on the bumpy banking at Montlhéry. For this run Eldridge took the wheel as George was still recovering from his injuries. The five kilometres record was raised to 110mph before radiator damage caused the session to be abandoned.

Back at the factory a new radiator and revised supercharger drive were fitted and by the end of December George Eyston had recovered enough to be able to take the wheel during a session at Montlhéry, where the shorter distance records were raised to over 114mph. It is suggested that it was always George's intention to raise the speeds gradually so as not to totally demoralise the Austin team, who were their main opposition. Had Austin dropped out of the chase the publicity value of any new records set by MGs would have been lessened. There were also lucrative payments on offer from suppliers, like the oil companies, whenever new records were set, and it was obviously useful not to reveal your full performance at one go.

Kimber was keen for an MG to be the first 750cc car to reach 120mph and for this to count as an international record it could not be undertaken at Montlhéry as that venue did not at that time have the necessary approval. The car was required to do two runs, one in each direction, and the average speed was the one that counted. Brooklands was approved for such runs, but was closed for the winter. It was therefore decided to make an attempt at Pendine Sands, a site that had been used by other record breakers. The difficulty of running one the sand was that conditions varied from day to day, and it was a matter of sitting it out until both the weather and the sand were just right; a frustrating business when all concerned had a living to earn.

The model of the proposed EX120 successor was started at home by Reg Jackson and then completed in the factory before wind tunnel testing..

Bert Denly sitting in the tight confines of the cockpit of EX127 with George Eyston standing alongside.

On Monday February 8th conditions were as right as they were likely to be at that time of the year, so the team scoured the beach for any obstructions and got ready for the first run. The car performed well and hand timing showed it had reached 126mph. However, the official timing equipment ran out of ink and the speed was not recorded. By the time they were ready to make a further attempt conditions had worsened and puddles were appearing on the sand. These caused extra drag that slowed the car appreciably. Nevertheless, the records for the flying start kilometre and mile were raised to just over 118mph, but not the 120mph they needed. The attempt was then abandoned and they returned home.

During the first test at Montlhéry, carried out at the time of the last EX120 record runs, EX127 with Eldridge at the wheel was found to overheat badly. The cure was thought to be a surface radiator as used at the time on aircraft. However, when Eldridge returned to Montlhéry to try the car he found that the bumpy track caused the radiator to crack and leak.

After the disappointment over the attempt to reach 120mph on British soil the car had a thorough overhaul, which must have included trying to remove loads of wet, salty sand. At the Whitsun meeting at Brooklands the car captured the Class H lap record at 112mph and returned there in September for the JCC 500-mile race where, despite not being designed for long-distance racing, it set a rapid pace before retiring when a piston failed.

Development of the C-type had led to the introduction of a cross-flow cylinder head but thus far EX127 had retained the original style with both inlet and exhaust ports placed on the same side of the engine. Prior to the next attempt to reach 120mph the engine was rebuilt using the cross-flow cylinder head and at the same time the cockpit was altered so as to totally enclose the driver beneath an aircraft-style canopy. There was to be a comprehensive attempt on a range of 750cc records so, in addition to EX127, the team that included George Eyston, Bert Denly, Reg Jackson and T.H. Wisdom, took one of the new supercharged J3s as well.

The cockpit alterations proved a step too far and George Eyston found driving the car very claustrophobic, so part of the canopy was cut away to improve the air circulation. There were other dramas with EX127 along the way, the most serious being a sudden and dramatic rise in oil consumption towards the end of the bid for the twelve-hour record. Denly had taken over the car for the last three-hour stint and having managed to come to grips with the high winds blowing across the track was circulating according to plan. Suddenly he noticed that the reserve oil tank was dry and that he had no oil pressure.

Having coasted into the pits he found that the sump too was almost empty. So the pit crew rapidly refilled both sump and tank with oil that they had kept warm over a stove and Denly went back on the track. However, that oil also rapidly disappeared and the team found themselves having to top up every few laps. The car was kept going until the end of twelve hours only because Eyston managed to break into the oil company store at the track to obtain fresh supplies. The fault turned out to be a broken rear bearing that was allowing oil through into the clutch housing, and by the time they stopped both the driver and the inside of the car were coated in Castrol R.

The result of the team's heroic efforts was a list of records for EX127 which included, on the first day, three at speeds in excess of 120mph. Long distance runs the following day saw EX127 take the three-hour record at 94.60mph, the six-hour record at 92.80mph and the twelve-hour at 86.67mph. Denly and Eyston shared the driving and they also took a number of other distance records. At the same time the J3 took its place in history by setting the 1000-mile record at 69.19mph, the 2000-kilometre at 69.95mph and the 24-hour at 70.61mph.

In October 1933 EX127 was transported once again to Montlhéry where it was joined for record-breaking attempts by a supercharged Austin Seven in the hands of Murray Jamieson, who was after the 750cc records already held by the MG. Although the two teams worked together when the cars were being prepared, a certain amount of subterfuge was necessary to ensure that the rivals did not know exactly what speed the other team had available from their car. The MG boys adopted the tactic of ignoring the Austin in practice, whilst timing the laps from the noise the Austin made as it passed over gaps in the concrete banking above their garage. When they practiced they never ran the entire lap flat out as they knew the circuit well enough to be able to estimate the potential from timing short bursts at full throttle.

Having fitted larger-section rear tyres to increase the overall gearing, when it came to the timed runs Denly raised the one mile and one kilometre records to over 128mph, and he felt the car still had something in hand. By now the height of the bodywork had been reduced and only someone of his short stature could be comfortable at the wheel. This was to be the last time the car ran under the control of George Eyston and Jimmy Palmes as it was sold by the factory to Bobby Kohlrausch, who took it to Germany. He entered the car for the Avusrennen in Berlin but had to retire, and he also found the body to be too small to be comfortable when used for road racing. The car was returned to Abingdon so the factory could build him another body for the car to use in other events, this in addition to the record-breaking body that he had already. The car was also fitted with a Q-type engine. Kohlrausch carried out further work on the car and used it for numerous events, with much success.

Record attempts continued and in May 1935 he raised the 750cc international records for the shorter distances of one kilometre and one mile to speeds above 130mph. In 1936 the crowning achievement for EX127 was a session on the new Frankfurt Autobahn where Kohlrausch raised the flying start mile record to the dizzy heights of 140.6mph. EX127 was eventually purchased by Mercedes-Benz in 1938, presumably for research purposes, and then disappeared from view.

EX127 was sold to R. (Bobby) Kohlrausch in 1934 and after just one event at the Avusrennen in Berlin, when he failed to finish, the car was returned to Abingdon as the cockpit was just too small for him. A brand new body was made for the car and painted in white, the German racing colour.

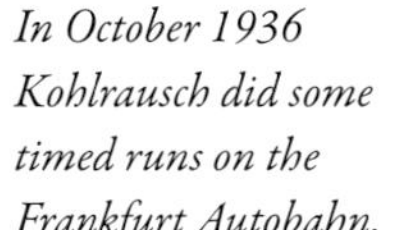

In October 1936 Kohlrausch did some timed runs on the Frankfurt Autobahn.

During record attempts on the Frankfurt Autobahn in October 1936 Bobby Kohlrausch established three international Class H 750cc records for one kilometre standing start at 82.72mph, one kilometre flying start at 140.51mph and one mile flying start at 140.6mph.

The J-Type Midgets

By 1932 the First World War had been over for 14 years, and for those young enough not to have been directly involved, memory of that dreadful conflict was starting to fade. The colourful excesses of the 1920s may have been over and the economic depression caused in the aftermath of the 1929 Wall Street Crash had cast its shadow, but at least the rise to power of the European fascists had yet to occur and talk of another war was still in the future. For those in work, or with sufficient private income, they were not bad times. Many roads had yet to be properly surfaced, but at least there were fewer cars, and those running them were still a privileged minority. Motoring was, however, starting to become more regulated. 1931 had seen the printing of the first Highway Code and the same year third party insurance became compulsory. It may not, as some have said, have been the golden age of motoring, but it was certainly not a bad time to enjoy driving an MG.

The J1/J2 engine was installed in the chassis before the body was fitted.

When Cecil Kimber decided in 1928 to move into producing a small sports car based on the chassis and running gear of the newly announced Morris Minor, he could not have known that this was destined to take the fledgling MG Car Company into the big league. Prior to the introduction of the £175 Midget, the cars sold by the Morris Garages had all been aimed at a different market. The sporting saloons and tourers they offered had been built

Factory picture of a J1 Tourer.

With hood up and all four side-screens in place the J1 Tourer kept all four occupants dry.

using the standard Morris rolling chassis, but were hand finished and fitted with special coachwork. This made the cars relatively expensive, the cheapest costing about twice as much as the new Midget. Also, in 1928 there were signs that what Kimber was really aiming to do was take the MG marque even further up-market. He had just announced a new six-cylinder model based around a chassis constructed purely for the MG and here he was aiming for Lagonda, Alvis and Bentley territory. Without the Midget, MG would undoubtedly have shared the same fate as some other companies in the difficult economic climate due to emerge over the next few years.

The success of the M-type Midget came about because it really was in a class of its own and created its own sector in the market. Yes, there were other small cars of similar appearance, an example being sporting versions of the Austin Seven. Also appealing to a similar type of buyer were some of the continental cyclecars. But none of these in Britain was anywhere near as successful in terms of overall sales. It is true to say that the Midget gave a new generation of budding sports car drivers the chance to buy a car that was cheap to run, that outperformed most family saloons with engines of twice the capacity, and that looked the part in terms of styling and sporting appeal. It was the popularity of the Midget amongst its younger owners that led to the formation of the MG Car Club and to the growing participation by the marque in sporting events such as trials and club racing.

Despite the sales success of the first Midget, its humble Morris Minor underpinnings compromised its suitability for further development of the range of MG Midgets, or for competition use. The power unit was not the trouble as this was capable of being

A restored J1 Tourer. (Photo Neill Bruce)

J1/J2 rolling chassis.

developed to produce a great deal more urge. The chassis was the limiting factor. Following the success of the Midget, the company had been forced in 1930 to transfer to new, larger premises at Abingdon. This move away from the Morris assembly plant at Cowley meant that no longer were the cars built on rolling chassis assembled by Morris. All MGs were now put together at Abingdon from components manufactured elsewhere; in the case of the six-cylinder 18/80 using a chassis specially made for them, rather than sourced from a Morris production car. This meant that it was not imperative that they continue to use the Morris chassis for the Midget if a viable alternative could be made at a competitive price.

If the M-type had been crucial to the survival and expansion of the MG Car Company, the model that succeeded it was to be just as important. The J-type Midget range came to public notice with the press announcement in August 1932 and, although the basic components of the new model had all been seen before, it was the overall package that made such an impact on the buying public. When almost every family car can now easily top 100mph and we all think nothing of driving hour after hour on motorways at 70mph, or more, remember just how slow was the average family car in the 1930s. Drivers of most of the underpowered Austin and Morris small saloons in use were happy to cruise at around 45mph. Then

J2 cutaway drawing.

along comes an announcement of an 850cc sports car priced at just £199.10s that a magazine had tested and found to have a top speed of 80mph. It is now assumed that the car used was, shall we say, well prepared before being handed to the journalists. A more representative speed for the average J2 straight off the line was probably a few miles-per-hour less than that. Nevertheless, the potential was there and any new J2 was still a quick car for its time.

To add to the undoubted appeal of all that performance was the attractive appearance of the new cars. One can suppose that the overall design of the two-seater J2 came about as much from evolution as from deliberate policy. After all, the M-type started out with the then-fashionable boat-tailed look and similar styling was used for the C-type competition car. The latter had adopted a twin hump scuttle as, in theory, this gave some lift to the airflow over the cockpit and a measure of protection to driver and passenger when travelling without a full windscreen. Competitors had quickly discovered that the best way to gain extra performance was to have the lightest of bodies and they started to chop off the pointed tail section. They also found that a larger fuel tank could be accommodated if it was placed across the back of the car behind the shortened body. Thus, for purely practical reasons, was evolved the archetypical MG shape: the traditional radiator ahead of a long bonnet, a double-humped scuttle housing a dashboard containing business-like instrumentation,

With the screen folded down the occupants needed to wear goggles.

Lowering the windscreen reduces wind resistance and increases top speed.

bodywork with just enough room to accommodate driver, passenger and a few possessions, and a large, rear-mounted fuel tank with the spare wheel neatly placed behind it – a 1930s design classic that in essence served MG until in 1955 the MGA brought streamlining to MG owners.

The J-type replaced not just the D-type, but also the now outdated two-seat Midget. The later D-type chassis was carried over to the new J-type range virtually unaltered. The engine, while retaining the same basic

J0251 build commenced in April 1932. This was the first J2 and the road test car that recorded a top speed of 80mph. The factory retained it until June 1933.

J0251 photographed with the hood up. There seem to have been a different pattern of side-screens on this car to those fitted to other J2s.

layout, was much improved, inheriting what had been learned from the work done to develop the C-type. The cross-flow cylinder head that had been seen to improve power output was used together with twin SU carburettors, as fitted to normally aspirated C-types. As previously, the revised engine had overhead valves actuated by rockers lifted by a camshaft mounted on the cylinder head and driven via a vertically mounted dynamo.

All the J-type models, except for the J4 sports/racing car, had the Wolseley four-speed gearbox with a remote unit that incorporated a fixing for the bracket taking the choke and slow-running control rods. The gearbox for MGs had the speedometer drive at the back and intermediate gear ratios of 3.58:1, 2.14:1 and 1.36:1. Initially the crankshaft ran in only two main bearings, a plain one at the back and a ball race at the front. When crankshafts began to fail because of both fatigue and excessive vibrations and flexing, an additional ball race was introduced at the front, without completely eliminating the problem. Most engine rebuilds that have been carried out in recent years will feature counterbalanced Phoenix crankshafts. An electron cast ribbed sump cooled the gallon of oil in the lubrication system. A coil and distributor provided ignition, with the J4 having twin

Factory picture of a J2 with the hood up.

J0512 has been restored in America and won a concours at Pebble Beach.

coils. A Petrolift initially fed fuel to the carburettors, but from J3434 the SU petrol pump was fitted. The rear axle was inherited from the earlier cars and was fitted with spiral bevel gears of 5.375:1 on the J1 and J2 and 4.78:1 on the J3. The J4 axle had straight-cut gears of 5.375:1 ratio, since with racing cars noise was less important than strength. The cable-operated braking system used 8-inch diameter drums with shrunk-on aluminium cooling fins.

The J1 models were a four-seat open Tourer and a Salonette, both very similar to those that had been fitted to the later D-types. The tourer was priced at £220 and the closed model at £255. As was then the fashion for sports cars, the tops of the doors on the open model were cut away to provide more elbowroom. The wings were the helmet-shaped type, like the D-type, for the J1 models, but lighter cycle wings of semi-circular profile were provided for the J2, J3 and J4 models. The ex-works price of the J2 was £199 10s, the J3 £299.10s and the J4 £445.

The standard colour scheme for the J1 models was black with leather upholstery in a choice of Apple Green,

J3092 has been restored with non-standard bucket seats.

The colour scheme of J3092 would have cost extra as the normal two-colour option was Saratoga Red and Carmine Red.

Tudor Brown, Deep Red, Cerulean Blue or Suede Grey. The roof and rear quarters of the Salonette were painted to match. The J2, J3 and J4 had a standard black finish with the same choice of leather upholstery. At extra cost, cars could be painted in two colours, although customers were warned this could delay delivery. The six colour schemes available were Dublin and Ulster Green, Cambridge Blue and Oxford Blue, Brooklands Grey and Abingdon Grey, Old Ivory and Light Fawn, Saratoga Red and Carmine Red and White and Ebony Black.

Instrumentation varied from model to model. The Tourer and Salonette retained the D-type Rotax FT74

The engine bay of a restored J2.

J3571 was fitted from new with swept wings.

The engine bay of J3571, a car fitted with swept wings.

central panel fitted with 3-inch 80mph speedometer and a 2-inch oil pressure gauge and matching ammeter. The J2 had a 5-inch diameter speedometer in front of the driver marked with engine revolutions in each gear and set within an octagonal surround. A panel of the same size, also with octagonal surround, was placed in front of the passenger and this contained 1.5-inch diameter oil pressure and ammeter gauges, plus the ignition switch. Up to chassis J3575 the octagonal bezels were painted black, as were the centre and edges of the instrument panel. From J3576 the bezels were chrome plated and all instruments had domed, not flat, glasses.

As an extra at total cost of £12.12s, new J2s could be ordered with de luxe equipment. This consisted of an 8-day clock, an Ashby steering wheel, stone guards for the headlamps, an oil thermometer, a bonnet strap, snap lever petrol cap, a stop/tail lamp and a radiator thermometer. Any number of these could be ordered separately if you did not want the whole package. Many buyers specified extra equipment for their new J2s and some who intended using them to enter trials had lower-ratio rear axle gearing to aid climbing hills in first gear.

A major visual change with the J2 came from chassis J3438. The separate cycle wings that had proved lightweight and practical for competition use were less effective at keeping driver and passenger free from road dirt and damp. From that chassis until the end of the production of the model the J2 was given flowing, swept wings of similar pattern to those also fitted to the six-cylinder L-Magna models. Although heavier and overtly less sporting, the new wings must have made the J2 a more practical everyday car. New brochures were printed, but the price remained at the headline-grabbing £199.10s.

R.E.A.L. Carriage Works fitted this four-seat body to a J-type chassis, possibly J0515 or J2083.

R.E.A.L. Carriage Works offered this two-seat body for £50. It is fitted here to possibly J0515 or J2083.

J-Type Special Bodied Cars

As was the case with the M-type, the J was available as a rolling chassis so that customers could have different coachwork fitted, and 23 left the Abingdon factory in this form. J0327 went to Meredith Coachcraft of Birmingham and was probably given one of their Trinity bodies featuring either two- or four-seat drophead or closed coachwork. Again University Motors offered their folding-head coupé for the J-chassis for a total of £295. The Carlton Carriage Company of Waldo Road, Willesden, London NW10 probably made these for them. Another coachbuilder involved was R.E.A.L Carriage Works of Popes Lane, London W5. That company offered a two-seater body for the J2 at £50 and probably also built cars for sale. There is also a picture of a four-seat tourer built by that firm, probably on J2083 or an unidentified J1 chassis.

J2 chassis J2411 was exported through University Motors to Karosserie O. Uhlik of Prague, with details appearing in the *MG Magazine* for November 1933, together with a picture of the car displayed alongside the coachbuilder's name board. Another exported J2 chassis exhibited at the 1933 Paris Motor Show had a coupé body by Belgian Van den Plas Coachbuilders. This was an altogether more elegant effort. Unlike the factory Salonette it did not have room for a back seat. J3475 went through University Motors to Stiles Limited and was fitted with one of the threesome bodies more usually seen on the F-Magna chassis. J3573 went to C.K. Andrews & Co. Of Swansea, but what bodywork it received is not recorded.

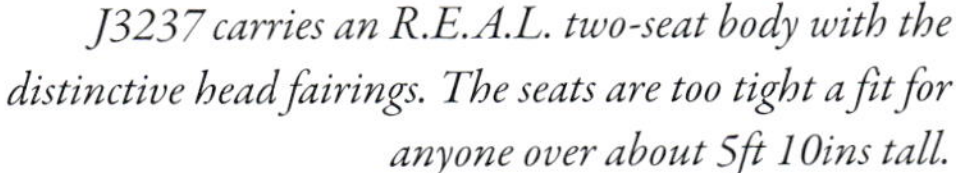

J3237 carries an R.E.A.L. two-seat body with the distinctive head fairings. The seats are too tight a fit for anyone over about 5ft 10ins tall.

THE R·E·A·L 'DEMON'

on a M.G. MIDGET SPEEDSTER Chassis

The REAL body on the M.G. Midget underslung chassis meets the demands of all M.G. enthusiasts who desire attractive sporting lines combined with safety and comfort.

The completely detachable air cushioned seats which are leather covered and adjustable, fit snugly to the body and make for absolute driving comfort. Headrests forming speed farings, a well shaped folding screen, a concealed hood, handy lockers in the doors, a detachable back, beautiful cellulose finish and extremely well shaped wings are other interesting innovations that make the REAL "DEMON" M.G. Midget an attractive speedy sports car from stem to stern

PRICE £225

Body £50. Chassis £175.

Catalogue detail for R.E.A.L. bodywork.

Advert for the University Motors drophead body as fitted to the J-chassis.

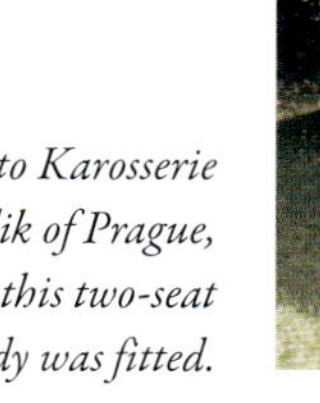

J2411 went to Karosserie O. Uhlik of Prague, where this two-seat closed body was fitted.

The cockpit of the body fitted by Karosserie O. Uhlik of Prague.

J3475 went through University Motors to Stiles Limited and was fitted with one of the threesome bodies, like this one on an F-type chassis.

J-chassis fitted with two-seat coupé body by Van den Plas of Belgium on display at the 1933 Paris Motor Show.

The J2 Midget In Motor Sport

Almost as soon as the J2 was in production examples began appearing in competitive events. A look through surviving chassis files and through programmes and results sheets reveals how high a proportion of the cars built saw some sort of competition use, even if only at weekends in small club events. In 2010 long-term J2 owner Mike Hawke published his second book on the J2, *How they Ran*, listing the competition efforts of 494 cars he could identify and up to 307 other possible J2 entries where he could not identify the car used. As total production was well below 2500 cars, this means that a fair proportion were used competitively,

J3280 was bought new for Doreen Evans and supplied in grey primer so it could later be painted in the blue chosen as the Belleview Garage colour for all the cars driven by the Evans family.

Doreen Evans driving J3280 in the 1934 Colmore Trophy Trial where she gained a second class award.

J2714 with A.W.F. Smith at the wheel in the 1933 Land's End Trial on his way to yet another premier award.

J3 driven by J.E.S. Jones in what was probably the 1934 Brighton-Beer Trial.

even allowing for any errors compiling the figures.

As examples of the type of use to which a great many J2s were subjected we can look at a couple of cars. J2005 was built in early December 1932, registered JB 552 and lent to Alan Hess for the NWLMC Gloucester Trial on 10th December and the MCC Exeter Trial on the 31st. He earned silver awards in both events. In 1933 he entered the car in more events, including the Colmore Trophy Trial where he was part of the class winning team. The car may well have been a perk of his job when he became editor of the *MG Magazine*.

A perhaps more typical example is J2056. This was a standard two-seat sports model painted red that was sold by the Eastbourne MG dealer to J. Hornsby, but by early 1934 was owned by J. Scott Hepburn of Glasgow, who in 1934 and 1935 proceeded to enter a great many events, mainly in Scotland.

Much the same story applies to most of the J2s for which the remaining records give details. Just how big an effect this model had on the British motor sport scene in the 1930s is not clear, but at that time the MG marque in general greatly swelled the entry lists.

W.J. 'Dickie' Green in J4227 during the 1934 Brighton-Beer Trial when he earned a first class award.

20

Route and Standard Times

April 19th p.m.		Miles
10.0	**VIRGINIA WATER**	
April 20th a.m.		
12.35	**DEPTFORD** (Check)	66¾
12.59	**Willoughby Hedge**	77
2.38	**TAUNTON** (Car Park)	120¼
4.12	**Taunton** (Depart)	
*5.17	**GRABHURST HILL** (Cars only)	148¾
5.37	**Porlock**	155¼
	Doverhay Hill (Motor Cycles only)	
6.03	**COUNTY GATE** (Check)	161½
6.17	**Lynmouth Bridge**	166¼
	LYNMOUTH HILL	
6.22	**STATION HILL** (Lynton)	167¾
6.25	**Barbrook Mill**	168¾
	BEGGARS' ROOST	
7.21	**South Molton**	187½

April 20th a.m.		Miles
8.25	**Stibbs Cross**	209
9.03	**Meddon Cross** (Main Road)	221¾
9.16	**DARRACOTT HILL**	226
10.19	**LAUNCESTON**	249½
11.49	**Launceston** (depart)	
p.m.		
12.51	**Wadebridge**	276½
12.58	**HUSTYN HILL**	278¾
1.17	**Junction with A.30** (6 miles west of Bodmin)	285
1.59	**PERRANPORTH**	302¾
2.09	**Perranporth** (Depart)	
2.18	**Trevellas Porth**	305½
	BLUEHILLS MINE	
3.07	**Hayle**	322
3.29	**Penzance** (Promenade)	329¼
3.59	**LAND'S END** (Finish)	339¼

N.B.—The Motor Cycle Route at County Gate totals 165¾ miles, and from thence to Land's End is 4¼ miles more than the mileages given above, which are the Car route mileages.

**The first car is due at Grabhurst at approximately 6.30 a.m.*

Walker & Co. (Printers) Ltd., 30 Gt. Russell Street, W.C.1.

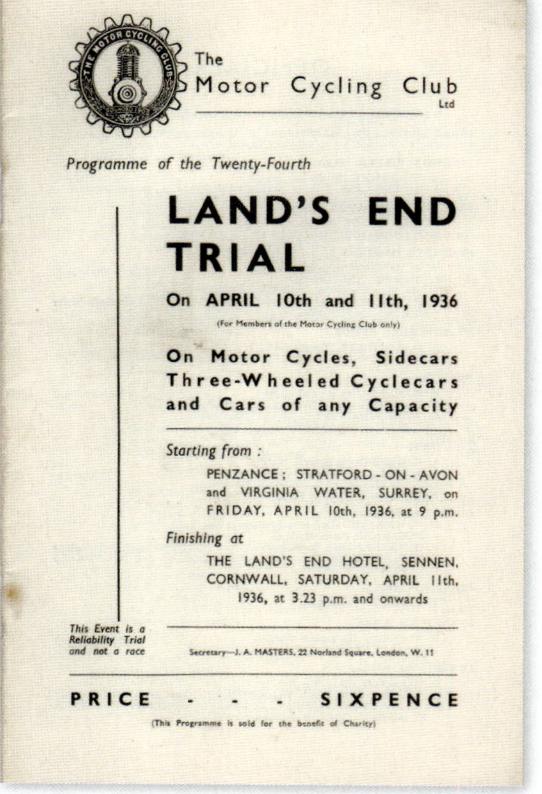

The Motor Cycling Club Ltd

Programme of the Twenty-Fourth

LAND'S END TRIAL

On APRIL 10th and 11th, 1936

(For Members of the Motor Cycling Club only)

On Motor Cycles, Sidecars Three-Wheeled Cyclecars and Cars of any Capacity

Starting from :

PENZANCE; STRATFORD - ON - AVON and VIRGINIA WATER, SURREY, on FRIDAY, APRIL 10th, 1936, at 9 p.m.

Finishing at

THE LAND'S END HOTEL, SENNEN, CORNWALL, SATURDAY, APRIL 11th, 1936, at 3.23 p.m. and onwards

This Event is a Reliability Trial and not a race

Secretary—J. A. MASTERS, 22 Norland Square, London, W. 11

PRICE - - - SIXPENCE

(This Programme is sold for the benefit of Charity)

Land's End Trial Route books.

J3 Midget

For many the J3 model is something of a mystery. Produced in small numbers and costing at £299.10s half as much again as a standard J2, the whole package is very much more than merely a J2 with a supercharger bolted on the front. Neither is it a road-going version of the J4. Initially an un-supercharged J4, the J5, was listed, but none were ever built and the model was dropped from the range in later catalogues and advertisements. Actually, the J3 should be regarded as a separate and very effective sports car in its own right. Of all the Midgets built at Abingdon in the 1930s the J3 must be one of the most rare and most desirable.

The J3 was expensive and any of the wealthy buyers would not have been disappointed at what they received for their money. The cars were built at Abingdon on a separate production line used solely for special orders. They were assembled from bare chassis and all the modifications were incorporated as the cars progressed down the line. A couple of men assigned to the task put together most of the car, but people from the racing shop did the engine assembly and supercharger installation.

From a study of the specification of a typical J3, bearing in mind that it is likely that no two were exactly the same, one can see why it made more sense to build these on a different line. Starting from a bare chassis, they were assembled with the different piping needed to supply an Autopulse fuel pump mounted on the bulkhead. There were stronger front road springs to counteract the extra weight of the supercharger and a more substantial front axle. The rear axle had higher-ratio final drive gears giving 16.4mph per 1000rpm in place of those used on a standard J2. There was also a stronger clutch and an additional support bracket for the gearbox to counteract the greater torque produced by the supercharged engine.

The body was the same as that used on the ordinary cars, but the fuel tank had a wider neck to take a racing filler cap. Inside the cockpit the upholstery and trim were as the cheaper model, but the dashboard layout incorporated a boost pressure gauge; this was probably the same with most J3s and they would also have had the extra instruments found on deluxe J2s. However, with most being built to special order, it is likely that the instrument layout varied from car to car. The brakes for the J3 were normally the 8-inch drums from the J2, but one car had 12-inch drums from new.

The heart of the J3 is the engine/supercharger installation. The factory designed a new, stronger crankshaft with larger diameter big-end bearings. This was not the fully counterbalanced shaft used in the J4, but was a lot stronger than that fitted to the J2. This special crankshaft had a reduced throw to take the engine capacity to 746cc, comfortably within the 750cc international racing class. The cylinder head was 3/32in thicker to increase the size of the combustion

Factory picture of a standard J3.

J3 Chassis detail pictures.

space and thus reduce the compression ratio from 6.2:1 to 5.2:1, necessary with a supercharged engine. The connecting rods were stronger and different pistons were used. Fitted with a Powerplus blower the power output was rather optimistically quoted in contemporary sources as 72bhp at 6000rpm, the 850cc engine in the standard car producing 36bhp at 5500rpm. However, even if the power was slightly less than that given above, the J3 was certainly a quick car.

In their road test published in May 1933, *Motor Sport* recorded a top speed well in excess of 80mph and acceleration to 60mph in about 17seconds. This may not sound fast now but in 1933 would have seen off almost all other small-capacity production road cars. They remarked on how quietly the engine and blower ran, although the exhaust note was strident above 3000rpm. Perhaps because of its high cost, sales of the J3 were slow and records show that the 22 cars were built and delivered over an 11-month period. All had cycle wings, except for the final car, which was fitted with swept wings from new and was only given cycle wings in recent years.

The J3 Midget In Motor Sport

The chassis numbers of the 22 cars built run from J3751 to J3772. Work on assembling another car, J3773, was commenced, but it was completed as a standard J2 and issued with the J2 chassis number J4425. There is an MG Car Company advert featuring the first place in the Ballybannon Hill Climb achieved in J2024 and describing the car as a J3. Perhaps it had acted as a guinea pig for the J3s offered for sale as it had been given a 750cc engine for the 1933 Monte Carlo Rally, from which the car retired. Assembling J3751, the first J3, began on 3rd November 1932 and a few days later it was delivered to Scottish Motor Traction, the Edinburgh MG dealers. The first owner was D. Harrison, but by the following year he had sold the car and the new owner was D. Donaldson. This second owner entered the J3 in the Edinburgh and District Motor Club Scottish Six-Days Trial, earning a silver cup, and with a pair of J2s driven by H.J. Stewart and Miss M. Dickson took the club team award. He entered a number of other events in 1933 and 1934 before selling the MG to F.G. Lomax, who was to own and actively campaign the car until the 1950s. He entered races, hill climbs and other speed events at locations as diverse as Southport Sands, Prescott and Brighton, with some success. Around 1960 the car went to A.J. Merrick, who fitted the single-seater body originally fitted to a Q-type Midget, QA0251, and entered the modified J3 in a few races before selling it in 1964.

J3752 was the University Motors demonstrator first registered to their salesman and noted racing driver, Hugh Hamilton. In 1933 Countess Pamela Moy, who lived in Baden-Baden, bought the car and in her hands it was placed first in class in the 1934 and 1936 Paris-St. Raphael Rallies. Her J3 was returned annually to Thomson and Taylor at Brooklands for servicing, and in 1935 the original Powerplus supercharger was replaced with a Marshall. She sold the car in 1936 and after the war it found its way to the United States via unrecorded owners in France and Mexico.

The first owner of J3755 was W.T. Platt, who took delivery late in 1932. His first event in the new J3 was the gruelling Monte Carlo Rally, and in this he shared the driving with A.W. Archer. Along with the majority of British competitors, they elected to start from John O'Groats and found driving conditions that year to be fairly demanding. Bitterly cold winds, snow, ice and temperatures often well below freezing made the journey across Europe something of an ordeal, especially in an open car with little or no heating. Nevertheless, the J3 made the finish in creditable 32nd place and in the Mont des Mules hill-climb Platt took first place in the 750cc class. 1933 was the last year the hill-climb was run in conjunction with the rally.

In the hands of its first owner J3755 continued to take an active role in motor sport. In the April 1933 MCC Land's End Trial Platt earned a silver award and the following month was presented with a first class award in the Sutton Coldfield & North Birmingham Automobile Club Vesey Cup Trial. In October 1934 an entry in the MCC Sporting Trial resulted in a bronze award, but that is the only other recorded success by Platt. By 1937 the J3 was in the hands of G. Highley and in April that year he took first place in the 50-mile Coronation Handicap run at the Southport Sand Race Meeting. He was obviously a serious competitor as by the following year he had fitted the car with an attractive single-seater body. At the May Southport meeting he notched up a number of good results: for the one-mile sprint he was first in 850cc class, second in the 1100cc and 1500cc classes and won the 10-lap handicap race. At the September meeting he improved his performance in the sprint, taking first place in the 850cc and 1100cc classes and second in both the 1500cc and unlimited classes. He was only third in the 10-lap handicap, probably because by now the officials had realised how fast his 750cc car could go, but he won the President's Cup Race and finished a whole lap ahead of the competition. He was to keep the car until 1939, when it was to pass through a number of owners before being bought by J.W. Dickie in 1964, later passing to Bob Dickie. It now carries a standard J3 body.

J3756 was completed at the end of December 1932 and registered by the factory as JB 1047. Later that month the J3 was driven to Montlhéry to take part in the record-breaking session arranged by George Eyston for EX127. In preparation for this the car was fitted with a special gearbox and rear engine mounting and the dashboard was given extra illumination for the gauges, a separate tachometer, a pump to pressurise the fuel tank and a firewall-mounted reserve oil tank to automatically replenish the sump. The J3 was stripped of all unnecessary weight: hood, windscreen, all mudguards except the rear one on the driver's side, and the headlights. A small, curved aero screen and a bank of

The front mounted supercharger distinguishes the J3 from the ordinary, much cheaper J2.

J3756 was built 7th December 1932 and was taken later that month to Montlhéry for an attempt on the International Class H 750cc records. Driven by Eyston, Denly and Wisdom, new 1000-mile SS, 2000km SS and 24-hour SS records were set at speeds of up to 70.61mph. The car was then tested by Motor Sport *magazine and entered for the 1934 Le Mans Race.*

auxiliary lights were fitted.

For the attempt with the J3 on the long-distance records, Bert Denly and T.H. Wisdom joined Eyston and, after a long wait for suitable weather, started the run on 19th December. The first session saw Eyston setting an average speed of 75mph, but the second with Wisdom at the wheel was halted on the far side of the track when the fuel supply failed. He had to push the car unaided to the pits where hasty repairs were made to the fuel pipe. The rest of the 24-hour run went better, with only about 15 minutes lost when the ignition system played up, and in the end the team took three records: 1000 miles at 69.19mph, 2000km at 69.95mph and 24-hours at 70.61mph.

On its return to Abingdon the car was sold for £120 to Tom Hollinrake, a young New Zealander who was working at the factory. He was allowed to overhaul the car in working hours, fitting a new supercharger and extra dashboard instruments. He used the car on the road for a while before being introduced by John Thornley to Louis Dreyfus, who wanted to buy an MG to drive at Le Mans. In the event, Dreyfus did not drive the car, but in the hands of Gordon Hendy and H. Dines Parker it completed 123 laps before a bearing failed. After this Hollinrake repurchased the car for £150 and exported the J3 to Australia

J3760 was completed in March 1933 with white paintwork, the German racing colour, and exported to the MG dealer, R.A.E. Birch. Bought by Dr. Börries Freiherr von Münchhausen in 1933 the car was entered in many events all over Germany. Münchhausen had a lot of success with the MG, gaining a number of first and second places in the 750cc class. However, in January 1934 he unfortunately had an accident in the car and was killed; following this the J3 was rebuilt and fitted with a new body. The car appears to have survived as in 1995 it

J3764 was sold new to R.A.E. Birch and exported to Germany.

was recorded as being in France and being rebuilt.

J3 chassis number J3761 was unique in that it was fitted from new with a Salonette body. No early history is recorded, but by 1939 it had been dismantled and after the war was rebuilt and fitted with a single-seater body, later replaced by one from J4004. Having suffered the indignity of being given a Ford engine in the late 1950s, the J3 was up for sale in 1962 with a PB power unit. It is now in America.

Quite a fair proportion of the J3 output seemed to have emigrated to the warmer Australian climate. In addition to those already mentioned, J3762, J3763, J3766, J3767, J3770 and J3771 also took the boat trip there. With the exception of J3766, all have survived.

Chassis J3765 was delivered to Graham & Roberts Limited in April 1933 and sold to Leslie F. Robson. The following month it was fitted at the factory with 12-inch brakes and duplex shock absorbers. Robson earned a silver medal and was first in the 750cc class in the E&DMS Six-days Trial. After entering the MSAC Experts Trial in October the J3 was fitted with some J4 parts and outside exhaust for the 1934 season. An entry in the SSCC Highland Two-day Trial earned a First Class Award. Robson had sold the J3 to a young man from South Africa who found it too fast and powerful for his driving skill, and after a trip through a hedge Robson bought the car back. Once repaired, it went to a friend of Robson's, Denny Tong, who lived in Lancaster with his mother. He entered a couple of Southport Sands events, but later Robson had it back and the next owners were the brothers Edward and Ian Gillett and their father. The car was swapped around between these owners right up to the war, being entered in a number of events.

P.B. Tanner, a keen trials enthusiast, purchased J3768 and entered the J3 in numerous events right up until the outbreak of war in 1939. The list of trophies gained in the great many major trials he entered is certainly impressive as it includes a number of first class and gold awards. By 1946 the car was owned by Fred Hill, the proprietor of Empire Garage, North London, and in his hands it continued its competition career. He was awarded gold medals in the 1951 and 1952 Land's End Trials and set a new course class record at the Tewin Water Sprint. In 1953 he had moved on to racing a Lotus VI called the Empire Special, and it is thought that initially he used the 750cc engine from the J3 to power this. Later the car was fitted with a J4 power unit. J3768 survives, fitted now with a supercharged 750cc engine.

J3770 was sold by the MG Car Company to A. Freeman for his entry in the BARC Inter-Club Meeting at Brooklands on 8th July 1933. He ran the J3 in four handicap races and in the Team Relay Handicap as part of the Brighton & Hove MC team. After this the car went to Walter E. Belgrave for his entry in the 1933 Alpine Trial, where he earned a Coupe de Glacier for being one of only three cars to incur no penalties and to lead his class home.

The final production car to be completed to J3 specification was J3772. This was built with swept wings and finished with two-tone grey paintwork. Initially used a factory demonstrator, it was then purchased by Miss E.V. Watson, who entered the car in a number of trials. She was a keen competitor and also later drove a PA, a six-cylinder NA and a BMW 328 in various events. She sold the car in the mid-1930s and after this it went through numerous owners and spent some time in America, before being restored in the late 1980s and fitted with cycle wings.

From this brief account of the eventful lives of some of the J3s, one can see that they were an important part of the MG story and worthy of being considered as a model in their own right and not just as slightly altered J2s.

The J4 Midget

The J4, the racing version of the J-type Midget, was only built in small numbers, and finding one for sale now would be difficult. However, quite a number of J2s have been rebuilt to approximate J4 specification and make exciting road cars. When the J4 was designed engine development was proceeding apace and by early 1933 all the six-cylinder engines built were of the much stronger, large-camshaft configuration. Obviously for racing it would have been desirable to have a three-bearing crankshaft and stronger valve gear for the four-cylinder J4, but development of that power unit was not well advanced and it was the ordinary J2 block that formed the basis of the J4 engine.

There are a considerable number of differences between the J2 and J4 models and as a result very few parts are interchangeable. The J4s were assembled using standard J2 chassis frames that had been modified as required to accept the different components. Stiffer road springs were used and these were bound with cord, in line with usual racing practice. Hartford 306M dampers were fitted. The steering had a Bishop Cam unit in place of the usual J2 Marles Weller box and there was a divided track rod, with special drop and steering arms fitted to a different front axle. The braking system had12-inch drums and could be adjusted from the driving seat. The 750cc engine had a counterbalanced crankshaft, special rods and pistons and a pumped cooling system. A Powerplus number 7 supercharger

The M.G. Midget J4 Supercharged and J5 Unsupercharged Models

The M.G. Midget J4 Model

Specification

ENGINE. Four-cylinder engine cast en bloc with the upper half of the crank chamber. Exceptionally sturdy two-bearing counterbalanced crankshaft. Overhead valves operated through fingers by overhead camshaft carried on detachable cylinder head, all to special M.G. design, with inlet ports on one side and exhaust ports on the other side to ensure rapid combustion. The latest type 14 mm. sparking plugs have also been adopted. Camshaft drive by spiral bevel gears and vertical shaft at front end of engine, incorporated in this arrangement being the dynamo. Special aluminium pistons with steel connecting rods of particular design are fitted, each piston having three rings. Lubrication of the engine has of necessity received very special consideration. It is, of course, pressure throughout, the circulation being effected by an extra large gear type pump. There is also a Tecalemit 100% oil filter fitted. The oil is carried in a large elektron sump having cooling fins and a capacity of approximately 1 gallon. Fitted to the side of the sump is an automatic float feed device, which is used to maintain a level of oil in the sump from an auxiliary oil tank in the dash, the capacity of the tank being about 15 pints.

GEARBOX. The straightforward gearbox is of the latest advanced design of the twin-top type. Bottom gear of the low emergency order, whilst the second, third and top are of the close ratio variety specially selected for high-speed performance. The gearbox ratios are as follows :—

Top	1 —1
Third	1.37—1
Second	1.86—1
First	2.69—1
Reverse	2.69—1

GEARBOX (Pre-selective). Under certain conditions of racing when quick gear changes are essential it is a very definite advantage if the car is fitted with a pre-selective gearbox. Therefore we are offering this type of gearbox as an optional fitment for an additional £25 on the racing models. The pre-selective gearbox is manufactured under Wilson patents. Gear change is effected by depressing and releasing the clutch pedal after the gear required has been selected. The change speed lever is mounted on a gearbox extension close handy for the left hand. The gearbox ratios are as follows :—

Top	1 —1
Third	1.36—1
Second	2.0 —1
First	3.4 —1
Reverse	5.07—1

CARBURETTERS. Two large S.U. semi-downdraught automatic piston type with hand mixture control. When, however, the Powerplus supercharger is fitted, then the carburetter is bolted on to the casing of the supercharger and feeds through the special M.G. induction system to the inlet manifold. This special induction manifold renders the engine extremely tractable at low speeds, without in the slightest interfering with its very large power output, the idea being to maintain the gas velocity by using a small diameter induction pipe when the engine is running with the throttle closed, whilst the larger induction pipe comes in when the throttle is open and the engine is turning over fast.

COOLING. The cooling on both supercharged and unsupercharged models is by a positively driven pump from the crankshaft. The radiator is of the film type with a chromium-plated brass shell of exclusive M.G. design.

TRANSMISSION. When a straightforward type gearbox is fitted, a two-plate dry clutch is used in conjunction with the four-speed gearbox and engine unit. The propeller shaft is of the Hardy Spicer type with all-metal universal joints, whilst the back axle is of straightforward design with straight bevel final drive and ratios to order from standard selection to suit requirements. In the case of the pre-selective gearbox the clutch is incorporated in the gearbox unit.

CHASSIS FRAME. This is of special underslung design, the floor line being only 11 in. from the ground. The frame is built with tubular cross members and has a tubular steel brace at the rear end, the design as a whole being an ideal combination of stiffness under normal conditions and ability to yield to heavy blows without injury. The low build gives remarkable road holding.
The chassis is lubricated by means of a Tecalemit grease gun, grouped nipples being used together with the necessary pipe lines in all places where connections would otherwise be inaccessible.

STEERING. Cam steering is used, whilst the steering column is adjustable for rake, and is fitted with a special racing type spring spoke steering wheel, having a thin rubber-covered rim, the diameter of which is 18 in. The latest M.G. (Patent pending) twin track steering is also incorporated.

SPRINGS. These are flat and underslung, both front and rear. All springs are anchored at the front end and mounted in a slide at the rear end, there being a maximum of resistance to any transverse movement or oscillation. In accordance with racing practice the springs are taped and bound with cord.

Page Four

Specification sheet issued for J4 and J5 models. None of the latter was ever built.

was fed by a single 1 5/8-inch SU carburettor and there were special inlet and exhaust manifolds, along with a side-mounted exhaust pipe with a Brooklands silencer. A scuttle-mounted reserve oil tank was fitted.

The considerable power produced by the 750cc engine was transmitted to the rear wheels through a twin-plate clutch, a cross-tube mounted ENV gearbox, a two-inch diameter prop-shaft and straight-cut final drive gears. Unlike the standard J2, the J4 body had no doors and twin bucket seats replaced the usual arrangement with a one-piece backrest. The fuel tank had a quick-release filler cap and there were twin SU petrol pumps, with a Hobson fuel level transmitter. The dashboard was deeper than the one on the road car and a row of seven Rotax toggle switches replaced the ordinary ignition/lighting switch. In addition to the usual tachometer, ammeter and clock, there were gauges for fuel and oil tank levels, supercharger boost and oil temperature and pressure. This was a proper racing car that had been carefully designed for the job in hand; even the tonneau cover was securely located by straps, rather than with the usual lift-a-dot fastenings. Bearing in mind the time it would have taken to build a J4, even at the final catalogued price of £495 one cannot see how they made much profit.

The range of instruments and equipment provided as standard was impressive, but nevertheless there were a few extras available, at a price. The October 1933 brochure covering both the K3 and J4 racing models lists a chronograph clock, 120mph speedometer on a special bracket for road use, wire gauze racing windscreen and a streamlined detachable tail section. One could also order the car finished in a non-standard colour, should the available wide selection not be to your liking. There

Factory pictures of a J4 with the standard body fitted.

were also optional rear axle ratios and supercharger sizes on offer.

The model had much success at international level and by 1934 was still providing good results as backup to the newer Q-type and at locations where the Q had yet to run.

The J4 Midget In Competition

In all just nine of the sports/racing J4 models were built, but these seem to have been used hard in events in Britain and Europe. The first, J4001, was completed early in 1933 and sold to Robert Th. Meyer in Vienna. In May 1933 he attempted to set new Hungarian National sports car and racing car speed records for Class H 750cc and succeeded in establishing new ones for standing and flying start at speeds of up to 90.4mph. The following month Meyer entered the ADAC Kesselbergrennen in Munich, coming home third in the 800cc sports car class. In September he was placed first in class at both the Ecce Homo Hill Climb and the Semmering-Rennen before selling the J4 at the end of 1933 to Walter Wustrow in Austria. He used the car extensively in Europe, with some success. At the end of 1935 he appears to have damaged the J4 and nothing has been heard of it since.

J4002 was built with a lightweight J4 body and ownership was retained by the MG Car Company. The first race was supposed to be the JCC International trophy with H.C. Hamilton as driver, but the car is listed as a non-starter. However he did start the next time, at the ADAC race at the Nürburgring, where he was first home in the 800cc class. He also enjoyed success at following events, including first in class and second overall in the 1933 Tourist Trophy Race. That was the time he was beaten by Nuvolari in the K3, in an event where the handicappers favoured the J4 but a bungled pit stop allowed the brilliant K3 driver past. In the following race, in Brno, Hamilton crashed out of third place and the J4 went back to Abingdon for a rebuild, including a new chassis. Now painted white, the car was lent for a year to Bobby Kohlrausch, who scored a number of notable successes, setting new class records. Fitted with the standard body from J4003 it was sold to Mrs Elwes, who used it in events for a couple of years, notching up class wins at speed trials. From 1937 until now it has been in the hands of many owners, but survives.

J4003 was sold new with standard J4 body to J.C. Elwes and road registered APG 291. It was driven in a number of Brooklands races during 1933 before Elwes shared the car with M.B. Watson in the 500-mile race in September. A crash killed Watson and car was not repaired until early 1935, when the body swap with J4002 took place. The car was sold in 1937 and used in competition until 1949 by a number of owners, and then appears to have been stripped of parts. Known to have survived.

J4004 was sold new to D.K. Mansell with a standard body painted blue and registration number OJ 9483. Mansell took part in a race at Donington Park in the first year that the circuit was used as a car rather than motorcycle venue. In the RAC Mannin Beg that year he finished second. In 1934 the J4 went to F.I. Allen, who competed throughout that year and also at the first BARC Brooklands meeting in 1935, before the car was sold. Subsequent owners entered the J4 in competitive events right up to 1954, when the car was broken up and advertised for sale, including the chassis. The registration number has since appeared on a J1 chassis fitted with a J4 style body.

J4005 The first owner was Louis Fontes, who used the car throughout 1933 and 1934, entering events at Donington Park, Southport Sands and the 1933 Ulster RAC Tourist Trophy, where he failed to finish. At the end of 1934 the car was sold. After that it passed through many owners and spent over 50 years in America before returning to England in 2001.

J4002 was built at first with a lightweight body for loan by the factory to Hugh Hamilton to race at Brooklands and in Europe. After a crash it was rebuilt at Abingdon and lent to Kohlrausch for a year. It is seen in these 1970s pictures after a rebuild by Colin Tiesche.

J4002 photographed here when it was lent to Bobby Kohlrausch for a year along with K3001. Both cars are painted white, accepted at that time to be the German national motor racing colour.

J4006 was built with a standard J4 body, painted blue, and then went to MG dealer B. Waterhouse and Sons of Bradford, who sold it to C. Hanson, registered KY 4963. The car then passed through many owners but was not raced until it appeared in three events at Goodwood in 1950. Geoff Coles used parts of J4006 for the blue car he raced, and crashed fatally at Snetterton in 1974. It is now rebuilt and in Germany.

J4007 was built with a standard body painted blue and went to Attwood's Garage, Stafford. It was raced by H.R. Attwood in events at Brooklands throughout 1933. He also took the J4 to Ulster for the Tourist Trophy Race, but was not qualified as a finisher. In 1935 Rex King-Clark purchased the car and in 1936 had it fitted with a single-seater body. He raced the car for that year and in 1937 The Cresta Motor Company advertised it for sale in *The Sports Car*. I.H. Nicholls bought the car for £200 and fitted an R-type engine and a pre-selector gearbox. He raced the car right up to the outbreak of war in 1939. By 1946 J.R. Carmichael owned the J4 and he entered Scottish events in 1948, 1949 and 1950. Nothing else is recorded until 1973 when the car was sold to Beer of Houghton to join a collection of other MGs.

J4008 was built in July 1933 with a standard body painted blue. And was exported to France for Ecurie Jacques Menier. The car was fitted with Q-type brake drums and placed on show at the Salon de l'Automobile, Paris, in October. With P. Maillard-Brune as driver, the J4 was extensively raced right up to 1936 when the Ecurie Menier closed down. The car survived the war and went to Germany in 1984.

J4009 had a standard body and went to T. Simister & Company, registration AMA 916. It was raced by T. Simister at Donington Park, Southport Sands and Brooklands in 1933, 1934 and 1935 before being sold. By 1965 the car had been dismantled and most of the parts gathered up and united with the logbook and a substitute chassis frame. In 1971 it went to the Beer of Houghton collection.

Specification J-Type

Wheelbase/ Track	7' 2"/3' 6"
Wheels/ Tyres	Side laced wire, Rudge type 2.50" x 19"
	J1, J2 & J3 4.00" x 19"
	J4 4.50" x 19"
Brake drum size	J1, J2, J3 8-inch (One J3 fitted 12 inch drums from new)
	J4 12-inch
Engine/ power output	J1 & J2 847cc/36bhp
	J3 & J4 746cc/between 55 and 70bhp, depending on tune
Gearbox	4-speed no synchromesh
Build dates	J1 27th July 1932 to 7th July 1933
	J2 27th July 1932 to 10th January 1934
	J3 3rd November 1932 to 27th July 1933
	J4 10th March 1933 to 28th July 1933
Cars produced	J1 open 262, Salonette 117
	J2 2061
	J3 22
	J4 9
	Chassis 23

The PA & PB Midgets

The comparison between the first small MG Midget, the M-type seen in the showrooms between 1929 and 1932, and the PA and PB models sold between 1934 and 1936, illustrates the advances made in a very short time. The M-type was a very nice little car that initially featured a slightly modified Morris Minor chassis fitted with a 1920s style sports body. Although the OHC engine initially had a power output of just 20bhp and was allied to a chassis designed with family motoring in mind rather than as the basis of a sports car, the company produced a vehicle that was immediate hit with those looking for a cheap car with an attractive appearance. Its minimal weight and small size ensured better performance than the average family saloon, but it was no firebrand. Improvements to the engine for competition use saw output with the later production examples increased to 27bhp.

Development work carried out when the 750cc version of the M-type engine was built for the 1931 C-type Montlhéry Midget produced the next step up in power. The 850cc M-type engine had made do with a single carburettor, but the smaller-capacity C-type engine had twin SU carburettors and a free-flow exhaust. The original arrangement left the inlet and exhaust manifolds on the same side of the cylinder head and in this form produced around 37bhp, nearly double the output of the first Midgets. To make the cars competitive, more power was really needed and this came initially from fitting

The lavish booklet issued for the PA launch.

The PA chassis was similar to the one used for the J-type, but was stronger and had an extension at the back to support the spare wheel. Twelve-inch diameter brake drums replaced the eight-inch ones used for the standard Midget road cars.

The substantial spare wheel carrier introduced with the PA had the additional benefit of protecting the car from rear impacts.

a supercharger, lifting output to 44bhp, and then by placing the inlet and exhaust on opposite sides of the head to produce a normally aspirated 45bhp, increasing to 53bhp with a supercharger. Work carried out for the 750cc power unit was incorporated into the standard 850cc engine fitted in 1932 to the M-type replacement, the J2 with around 36bhp. So what was basically the same engine as had given just 20bhp in the first Midgets now had 85% more power. However, this revealed the weakness of the two-bearing standard crankshaft and there were many instances of failure in service, with consequent warranty claims.

Progressive improvements to both the four-cylinder and six-cylinder MG models continued apace. Weaknesses in the now more highly tuned 850cc engine prompted a complete reworking of the unit by the time the successor to the J2, the PA Midget, was announced to the public in March 1934. The press release spoke of a car produced to meet the needs of the sporting owner. A greater degree of reliability and safety was promised and it was said that the new model was suited to the most strenuous events. Much was made in the publicity issued by the MG Car Company of the revised cylinder head with a much more robust valve train, and that

The prototype PA. In production the sidelights were changed to ones that were octagonal in shape, the tonneau cover had three, not two, studs each side and the rear wings did not protrude below the bottom of the running boards.

DE LUXE EXTRA EQUIPMENT

	£	s.	d.
Bluemel "Malcolm Campbell" or "Ashby" Steering Wheel	1	1	0
Eight-day Clock	1	17	6
Dash type Radiator Thermometer	1	8	6
Dash type Oil Thermometer	1	8	6
Bonnet Strap and Fittings	1	5	0
Quick Filler Cap for Radiator		15	6
Quick Filler Cap for Petrol Tank		15	6
Head Lamp Stone Guards	2	3	0

The de luxe equipment (listed above) ordered with the car is available at the inclusive figure of £10 : 0 : 0, including fitting. Individual items may be had at the figures quoted, including fitting.

	£	s.	d.
D.W.S. Four Wheel Jacking System	5	5	0

Complete list of extras may be had on application.

COLOUR FINISHES

Exterior	*Body*	*Wings*	*Upholstery*
Black/Green	Black	Black	Apple Green
Black/Blue	Black	Black	Cerulean Blue
Black Red	Black	Black	Deep Red
* Ulster Green Dublin Green	Dublin Green	Ulster Green	Apple Green
Oxford Blue Cambridge Blue	Cambridge Blue	Oxford Blue	Cerulean Blue
Carmine Red Saratoga Red	Saratoga Red	Carmine Red	Deep Red

* In the case of duotone colours the darker shade is listed first. Carpets and hoods are black on all models.

Every precaution has been taken to ensure accuracy of this specification, the right however is reserved to vary it without notice. March, 1934.

Price list of available extras and a chart showing the range of colour schemes on offer.

The PA Tourer could carry four people, but when fully loaded performance suffered.

This picture is of the prototype PA Tourer shows the side-screens that protected the occupants from the worst of the weather. Again, production cars had three studs each side to attach the hood to the body.

A PA production model photographed at a location near to the factory.

Announcement leaflet produced for the 1934 London Motor Show.

Detail from PA catalogue.

the engine produced more power. Actually the stated output was virtually the same as the J2 engine managed. Unlike the six-cylinder version of the revised engine, the P-type engine was not fitted with a water pump. The front bevel gear housing has the hole where the pump would have been fitted, but with the PA/PB this mere has a covering plate. Supercharged cars would benefit from having a pump fitted. Early PAs had a Marles Weller steering box, but from chassis PA1287 a Bishops Cam box was specified. The prop-shaft universal joint was changed at chassis PA1755 to the Hardy Spicer type.

Despite not increasing power, the modifications produced a smoother and much more robust engine. Initially the PA blocks had a single breather, but the pattern was later changed to two breathers and it was this style that was altered for use in PBs, giving us a total of three different P-type blocks. A stronger

The seats in a restored PA Tourer.

The revised dashboard fitted to the PB models. The veneer was now burr walnut and there was a speedometer fitted in the centre taking the place of the odometer panel on PA dashboards. The rev-counter ahead of the driver no longer had markings for the road speeds in third and fourth gears. To the right of the steering column is the knob to select the reserve supply of fuel.

With the bonnet lifted there was easy access to the engine and all the ancillary components. Oiling nipples for the chassis lubrication points are conveniently placed on both sides of the bulkhead.

Posed period photograph of a PA and the camping trailer it could tow.

One P-type chassis ended up being used in a police driving school and is now often on display in the museum at Gaydon.

clutch and revised gearbox were a real advance that made the P-type Midget a more usable everyday car that was also better able to withstand hard use by enthusiastic owners. The PA ratios were (with J2 ratios in brackets) 4.18:1 (3.58:1), 2.32 (2.14) and 1.36 (1.36) in intermediate gears and axle ratio 4.18:1 (3.58:1). It seems that fitting the lower final drive ratio was an attempt to counteract the increased weight of the P-type over the previous model. What was never recorded at the time was how much fitting swept wings had affected J2 performance.

Perhaps the adoption of the swept wings first introduced with the last of the J2s had more appeal in the showroom than the revised mechanical specification. Following a seven-inch increase in the car's overall length, there was slightly more space for driver and passenger, while the wooden instrument panel veneered in American Sequoia and fitted with better instruments was another improvement. Other changes, like the stronger windscreen, Trafficator direction indicator arms and better mounting for the spare wheel, may not have been noticed at first glance, but were welcome nevertheless.

When the J2 was introduced in 1932 the big selling point emphasised in all the magazine reports was that for just £199 10s you could buy a car capable of 80mph. It was true that the carefully prepared test cars achieved this, but many owners found that their J2s struggled to match that speed. With the P-type no such claims were made. The car was heavier and the swept wings produced more drag, so the magazines found that the top speeds recorded over the standard measured quarter-mile distance were in the region of 75-76mph. However, the improvements with the new model meant that the car felt less stressed at cruising speeds around 55-60mph, making longer journeys more comfortable. The important change was the replacement of the 8-inch brake drums used on previous Midgets with the larger 12-inch diameter ones already fitted to the six-cylinder models. This gave the car really efficient braking, justifying the MG Car Company's Safety Fast slogan.

The main point of a sports car, apart from its appearance, was that it should be better to drive than the average saloon, and the 1930s MG Midgets were considerably quicker than the average 8, 9 or 10hp Austin or Morris family models. However, many owners still wanted more power and at that time supercharging was seen as the way to achieve this. There were bolt-on supercharger kits for the P-type available from various sources. Of course, very little in life comes free, and supercharging an engine to obtain more power had drawbacks. The main one was the cost. In 1934 a Zoller supercharger kit for a PA or PB Midget was priced at £27, with a further £6 10s for fitting. This may not sound much now, but as the Midgets brand new were by then just £220 the kit alone added

This restored PB Tourer is finished in the same Ulster Green and Dublin Green colour scheme as it had when it left the factory. The hood replicates the original design.

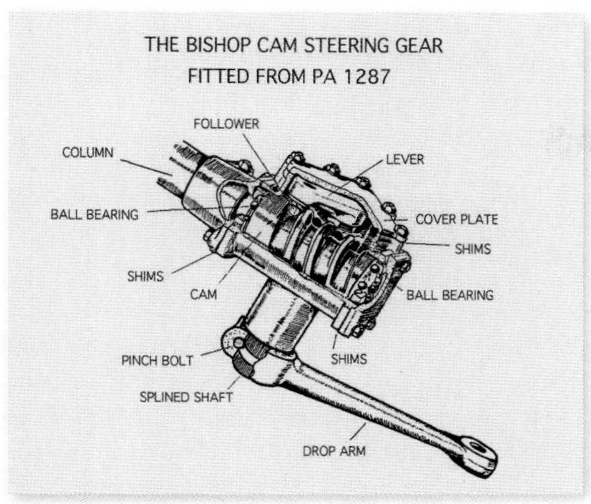

The Bishops Cam steering box fitted to the sports/racing J4 model and all Midgets after PA 1287.

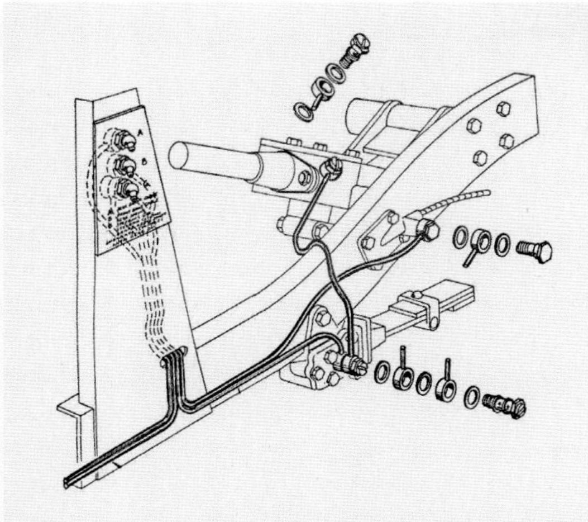

Lubrication pipes for the front of P-type chassis.

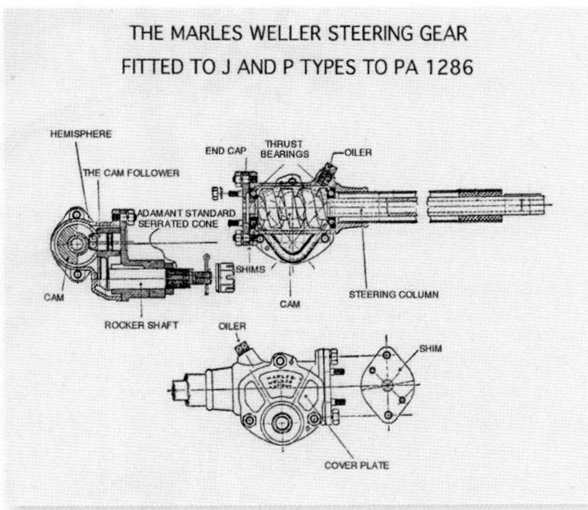

The Marles Weller steering box fitted to all Midgets up to PA 1286, except the J4.

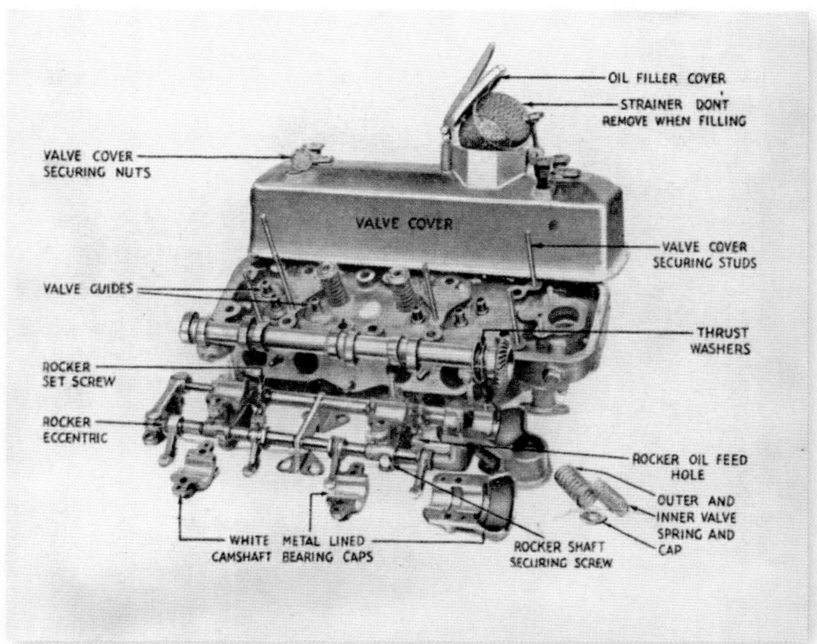

Exploded view of the typical layout of the OHC cylinder head.

over twelve per cent to the price of the car, in current terms about £4000. The Marshall supercharger was also offered in kit form for fitting to P-types. This cost £32, plus an extra £3 3s if you specified a separate pump to provide an oil feed to the supercharger, rather than relying on a drip-feed arrangement. Supercharged PAs were said by the manufacturer to be able to reach a maximum speed of over 85mph, with improved acceleration throughout the range.

A more cost-effective way for the MG Car Company to increase power was to enlarge engine capacity and this was the route taken for the P-type. After some 1,900 PA models of all types had been built, a revised power unit was introduced with a strengthened two-breather block bored out to take 60mm diameter pistons, increasing capacity to 939cc. Power went up from 36bhp to 43bhp and higher-ratio intermediate gears were used in a revised gearbox, but the PA ratios were available if the buyer specified these.

Although the PA was still available at a reduced price it proved difficult to sell. Strangely, the six-months guarantee started when cars left the factory and any still in the dealers' stock had to be returned to the factory for inspection before a fresh warranty was issued. In December 1935 a batch of 25 unsold PAs were converted to PB specification and given PB chassis numbers.

The PB enjoyed improved acceleration. A magazine test car recorded a time of just over 16secs to reach 50mph, four seconds quicker than the PA previously tested. The altered gear ratios also helped overtaking by allowed higher speeds to be reached in the two lowest gears. Other revisions made for the PB were the inclusion of a separate speedometer in the centre of the dashboard, now burr walnut veneered, replacing the odometer display on the PA. This was much better than relying on a tachometer with markings for road speeds in each gear. There was also a better clutch and to identify the new model the radiator grille was given vertical slats. This final version of the OHC Midgets was thus the best suited of all to being used as everyday transport. Much progress had definitely been made in only a very few years.

A road test printed in *The Autocar* began by saying that it was a car the journalists themselves wanted to own. They thought that it would be difficult for anyone not to be enthusiastic about a vehicle that could cover the ground about as quickly as any other car on the market and more speedily than most. A look through surviving chassis files reveals that the average P-type was not particularly reliable and one wonders what a current new car buyer would think of having to return their car to the factory for some repairs and that the guarantee covered parts, but not labour. There was a particular problem with the side-laced wire wheels. These had been built with the ends of the spokes protruding into the side of the wheel well. Fitting the usual rubber strip in the centre did not help, as it did not cover the sides of the well, so owners were told to remove the tyre and tube, file the ends of the spokes flush, and fit a new inner tube. The factory maintained a stock of modified wheels for those owners able to call in for the repair. PB production stopped on 13th February 1936 with chassis number PB 0775.

So what of the last, and arguably the best, of the OHC Midgets today? Prices asked for restored examples are considerable and the cost of restoring a neglected example is correspondingly high. So are they worth looking at? One has to say at the outset that there is one inherent downside with all the early Midgets, and that is their small size. People generally are both taller, and unfortunately often wider, than seemed to have been normal in the early 1930s. Once you manage to get into the P-type, especially with the hood up, the bench seats have enough adjustment to accommodate six-footers. On the other hand, the whole process is a challenge for those no longer as agile as they used to be. It may be that this is a case of 'try one before you buy one' to avoid disappointment, perhaps after carrying out a long and expensive rebuild.

On the plus side there is the sheer joy of trying to extract the maximum performance from a small and agile sports car. The engine thrives on high revs and the chassis enables spirited progress, especially on winding side roads provided these are well surfaced. There is much satisfaction to be obtained from getting gear changes right, even though for those more used to modern synchromesh gearboxes this can take some learning. There is also the enjoyment to come from just owning and looking at such an appealing car. Park one anywhere and you are almost guaranteed to attract favourable comments.

PB0682 was originally black with red trim and was one of the PBs supplied new to the Kent police.

A PA Airline Coupé on the MG stand at the motor show.

PA/PB Airline Coupés

When the P-type was announced in March 1934 initially only the open two-seater sports and a four-seater tourer were listed in the catalogue as being available. The previous Midgets had been sold also as small saloons, called Salonettes, so it was not surprising that a couple of months after the initial press release details of a closed version of the new P-type appeared in the magazines. The small saloon car was quite unlike any previous MG as it featured an up-to-the-minute design cashing in on the then current preoccupation with streamlining. Called an Airline Coupé, it was the work of a talented designer

Studio picture of a PA Airline Coupé.

The distinctive styling of the Airline Coupé body evoked the then current fashion of streamlining, but was somewhat at odds with the upright shape of the front of the car.

called Henry William Allingham.

Born 11th May 1882, to artistic parents, his father was a poet and magazine editor and his mother the well-known watercolour painter, Helen Allingham. It is therefore not surprising that Henry should exhibit a flair for design. Having benefitted from an engineering education at University College, Henry then went to Australia for a two-year apprenticeship where he worked on the pumps used to lift water from boreholes. On his return to England, thanks to a family connection, he was able to spend some months at Reynold chain factory in Manchester where he improved his engineering skills. He then crossed the Atlantic to America to learn about making Morse Chain and on return to England was employed to set up a new department to manufacture them at Westinghouse.

In 1921, after service with the Ministry of Munitions during the First World War, Henry became a director of the coachbuilders Chalmer and Hoyle at 41 Charing Cross Road. Initially the company

A restored P-type Airline Coupé finished in one of the standard range of two-tone colour schemes.

developed standardised car bodies for sale to vehicle manufacturers and this was so successful they had to take on extra space in a factory at Weybridge. One of their customers was Morris Motors, for whom they built closed saloon bodies for the Oxford model. They also branched out into boat building and the construction of bus bodies.

By the 1930s Henry had left the coachbuilder to set himself up as an independent designer working from offices in Central London. It was here that he devised the Airline body fitted to the P-type and to the six-cylinder N-type chassis. He also designed a two/four-seater body for the larger model, called at the time the Airline Convertible. Although he had the Hoyle connection, the Airline saloon bodies were actually built by the usual MG Car Company coachbuilder, Carbodies of Coventry Limited.

The Airline body construction followed the standard 1930s practice: an ash frame panelled in metal and, for additional strength there were steel windscreen pillars that went right down to bolt to the chassis frame. As had been the case with the previous closed Midgets, the sunshine roof incorporated small inset windows to bring more light into the cockpit. In the doors were sliding glass side windows which left space to accommodate recesses in the trim panels for additional elbowroom and also for the neat armrests. Room for some luggage was provided behind the pair of leather-covered bucket seats and the spare wheel was recessed into the sloping rear body panel.

The engine bay of a restored Airline Coupé.

Veneered and polished woodwork, plus good quality carpets, gave the interior an up-market appearance and the catalogue listed an attractive range of exterior colour finishes with cockpit trim to match. Unlike the two-seater where wheels were painted aluminium as standard, the Airline buyers had the choice of black, aluminium or red, blue, green or grey wheels. At an extra four guineas Ace aluminium wheel discs could be specified to avoid the chore of cleaning all those spokes.

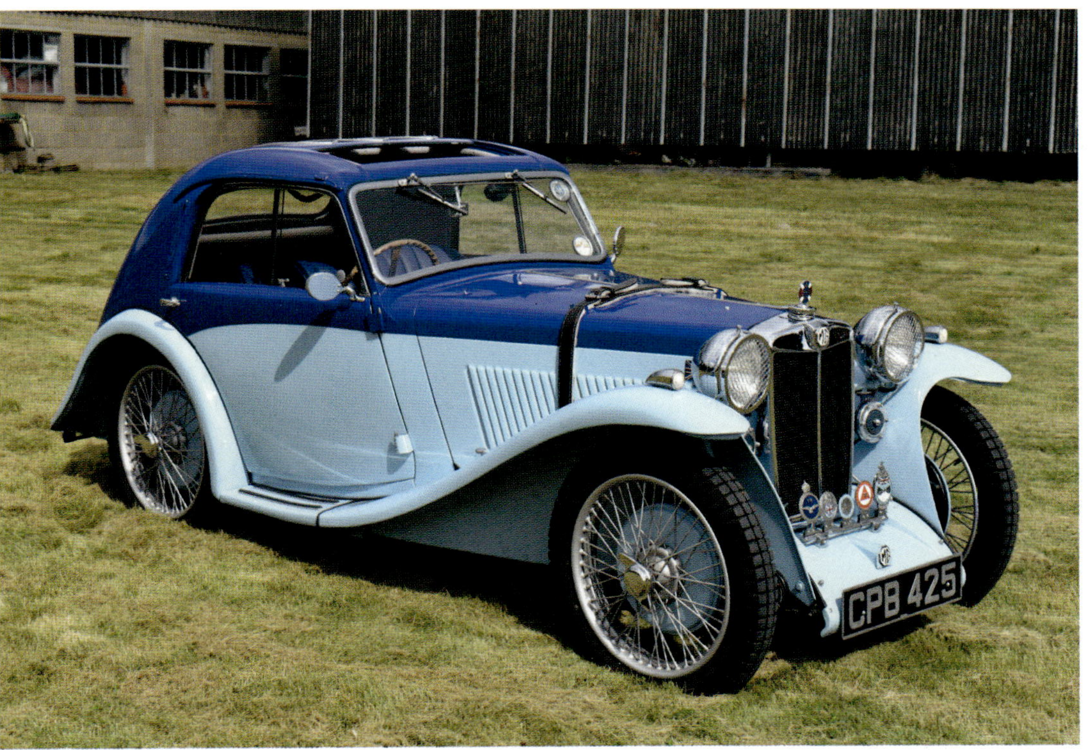

This Airline Coupé has been fitted with a number of period extras, stone guards for the headlights, union jack badges on the sides of the bonnet and a bonnet strap.

The Airline Coupé body attracts a lot of attention whenever the car appears at MG meetings.

Other additional equipment that could be ordered included an 8-day clock, dashboard water temperature gauges for oil and water, a bonnet strap, quick filler radiator and petrol tank caps, headlamp stone-guards, built-in jacking system and a second spare wheel. Adding that little lot would add a not inconsiderable £19 8s 6d to the £290 purchase price. The catalogue mentions that the Airline was produced under the supervision of H.W. Allingham and that, unlike cars with any other form of coachbuilt special body, the same guarantee as was given by The MG Car Company for the chassis applied to the bodywork from Carbodies.

The dashboard of this car has extra dials by the reserve fuel knob and a clock in the centre. The Brooklands steering wheel was a popular accessory.

The Abbey Coachworks P-type body was striking to look at, but it seems that few others, if any at all, were built.

PA/PB Special Bodies

A flyer issued in Switzerland for a special-bodied P-type.

As was usual in the 1930s, the PA/PB rolling chassis were sold to allow customers to have a coachbuilder fit a different style of body. During two years of production 57 rolling chassis were sold. For the home market the University Motors body was offered on the P-type chassis, but it seems unlikely any were built as they were expensive at £75 more than the standard car, and the bodywork better suited the six-cylinder chassis. There is also a 1936 *Autocar* advert for a Thomson and Taylor P-type special, but no clue whether this was built on a new, or used chassis.

The majority of the chassis went abroad, perhaps some as CKD kits. So as to protect local industry, in many countries import taxes on complete cars were higher than on components. Australia was a prime example, and there local coachbuilders constructed bodies that often resembled the standard factory offerings. However, C.F.S. Aspinall of Melbourne made distinctive all-steel bodies for Lanes Motors, the MG agent for that part of Australia. Some of their cars have survived.

Another good market for MGs was Switzerland, where import taxes were again heavy on imported cars. Sportscar A.G. in Zurich was the main MG agent for the country and even produced their own catalogue for MGs. Some models looked identical to the standard product, but nevertheless may have been built locally. Others exhibited a more radical approach, with the front wings incorporating running boards.

The P-type chassis fitted with a body built locally for sale in Switzerland through Sportscar A.G. possibly by Hanni coachbuilders.

This was either the same P-type as in the earlier picture fitted with spats for the rear wheels and a sloping radiator grille, or another P-type chassis with a body made by same coachbuilders.

PA/PB In Motor Sport

Like the other MG sports cars, owners of P-types soon began using them to enter production car trials, rallies and other speed events. Additionally, the MG factory supported the Cream Cracker and Musketeer trials teams that used at first the PA and later the PB, and these were successfully adapted to make them the cars to beat. As most of the modifications made for these teams by the factory consisted of removing many creature comforts to reduce weight, private owners needing to use their cars every day usually took a less drastic route. Low-pressure supercharging did not make the cars any less suited to normal use and was a popular modification. However, for some events this placed cars in the next class and running against larger-capacity rivals. Mild engine tuning and adapting the carrier to take twin spare wheels fitted with tyres that had deeper treads for the hill sections did not incur such penalties.

The Cream Cracker team, and later the Musketeers, were factory supported, although usually the cars were

The owner of this PA, Mr. Rippon, entered it in the 1936 Blackpool Rally.

The MG team photographed at the North West London Motor Club Team Trial in 1934. This was the start at Hartland, North Devon, with Toulmin in his PA with the cream and brown stripes leading the other two team cars.

sold to the drivers at the start of the season and bought back at the end of the year. The Cream Cracker cars made their first appearance wearing the MG cream and brown colour scheme for the 1935 Land's End Trial. Although this was the debut for the team of newly painted P-type Midgets, support for these cars by the factory had been evident well before this. Two of the members of the team, J. Maurice Toulmin and R.A. 'Mac' Macdermid, had privately bought their cars early in 1934 and the third team member, Jack A.

The very successful 1936 PB Cream Cracker team.

Toulmin climbing the steep hill at Rushmere driving his Cream Cracker PA.

Bastock, purchased his in that September. At first the cars remained in their original colours, two painted blue and one green, although later they had brown and cream stripes along the sides of the bonnets to identify them as being in an MG team. As they were still fitted with the heavy swept wings they were not as successful as expected and the cars were all returned to the factory for comprehensive modification before competing in the Exeter Trial at the end of 1934.

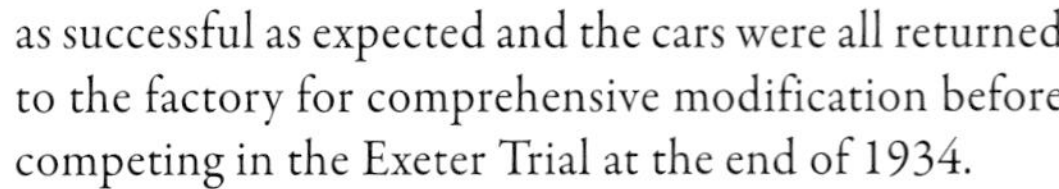

Cycle wings replaced the swept wings and they were fitted with lightweight aluminium bonnets, the lighter 8-inch brake gear and locked differentials. Much of the equipment, such as hoods, windscreens and side-screens, was discarded. Thus modified, the cars were more successful and took two first-class awards and one second-class award on the Exeter Trial. When they were returned to Abingdon to be prepared for the 1935 Land's End Trial it was decided to call the team Cream Crackers and to repaint the cars cream with brown wings, front apron, scuttle and bonnet top.

The ex-Toulmin/C.A.N. May Cream Cracker photographed in later years.

By the end of 1935, the factory had replaced the PAs with a team of three PBs, JB 7521, driven by Toulmin, JB 7524 for Ken Crawford and JB 7525 for J.E.S. Jones. The lessons had been well learned and the new cars, although similar in appearance to the earlier PAs, were more powerful, lighter and altogether more effective. In this form the cars enjoyed considerable success, which was exploited to the full in contemporary company advertising promoting the sale of standard cars.

Although out-and-out circuit racing was more the preserve of the cars built with this type of competition in mind, P-types were used by their owners in many

Betty Haig with her PB after the 1938 Paris to St Raphael rally where she was placed second overall.

speed events, like those organised by the car clubs at venues such as Brooklands. The factory entered a team of three PA Midgets in the 1935 Le Mans Race driven by a team of experienced lady drivers. There was also another PA in that race, privately run. Ever since, PA and PB Midgets have been entered by successive generations of owners in races, trials and in other competitive events run by the MCC, VSCC, and other car clubs. P-type chassis and running gear have also formed the basis of many MG specials built with competition in mind in the 1930s and also after the war, some of which have been very fast and successful.

Betty Haig kept her PB for many years and is seen here at an event in the 1970s.

Specification P-Types

Wheelbase/track	7' 3⅛"/3' 6"	
Suspension	Leaf springs front and back	
Wheels/tyres	Side-laced Rudge type 2.50" x 19"/4.00"x19"	
Brake drum size	12 inch	
Engine/ power output	PA 847cc/36 bhp	
	PB 939cc/43 bhp	
Gearbox	4-speed no synchromesh	
Build dates	PA 31st January 1934 to 22nd July 1935	
	PB 22nd July 1935 to 13th February 1936	
Cars built	PA two-seater	1396
	PA four-seater	498
	PA Airline Coupé	28
	PB two-seater	408
	PB four-seater	99
	PB Airline Coupé	14
	Chassis	57
	Total	**2500**

The Q-Type Midget

A cut-away of the Q-type drawn for when the model was announced to the press.

Early in 1934 The MG Car Company announced a new four-cylinder racing car, the Q-type, to replace the J4. Having had a season of successes with the K3 Magnette, they provided the new QA Midget with a chassis of the same wheelbase as the K3 and utilising the 4-inch chassis side members of the K-series cars, and the track at 3ft 9in was the same as used on the NA model. N-type axles, steering and brake gear were fitted, but with up-rated brake drums.

The four-cylinder, three main bearing P-type engine formed the basis of the power unit. Fitting a short-stroke 73mm crank produced a capacity of 746cc whilst a specially designed Zoller Q4 supercharger driven from the front of the crankshaft delivered a boost of just under 30psi. The claimed power output was 113bhp at 7200rpm. The gearbox was an ENV pre-selector unit and the flywheel incorporated a novel feature comprising a two-plate clutch without external actuating mechanism designed to protect the gearbox and final drive by slipping when a specific torque level was reached. The Q-type was fitted with a lightweight two-seater body with pointed tail and was really a four-cylinder version of the 1934 K3 Magnette. The engine produced only slightly less power than the six-cylinder K3 and the vehicle weighed less so the overall package was extremely quick.

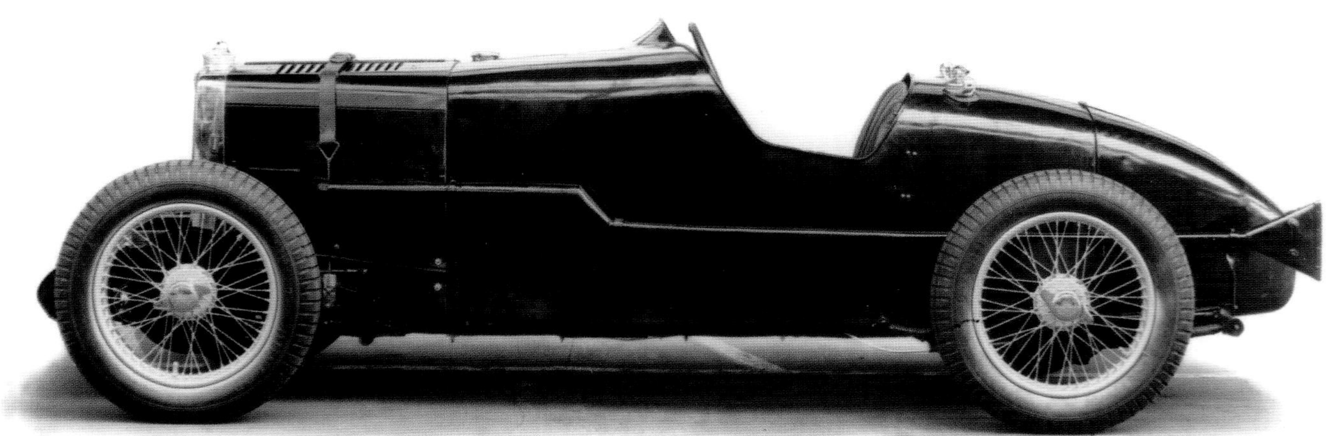

The lightweight body fitted to the Q-type chassis was similar to those fitted to the 1934 K3s.

At the Brooklands Whitsun Meeting on 21st May 1934 Bill Everitt entered the first Q-type, and on his first outing with the car he won the Fourth Merrow Mountain Handicap and in so doing broke the Brooklands Class H Mountain Lap Record with a speed of 69.97mph. Despite this success, the handling of the Q-type was not as much of an improvement over the J4 as had been hoped. However, for a car with a reputation of being a brute it is surprising that it seems to have reacted well to a delicate touch, as in their Q-types Doreen Evans and Dorothy Stanley-Turner, both petite young ladies, achieved several notable well-driven victories over their male counterparts.

The shortcomings of the chassis led directly to the introduction of the all independently sprung R-type the following year and no further development of the car took place at the MG factory during 1934, apart from improvements to the lubrication of the supercharger and alterations to the cooling system to prevent the overheating and cylinder head cracking, which plagued the standard engine. However, private tuners did a lot of work on the model, with Wilkie Wilkinson at Bellevue Garages modifying QA0254 to single-seater form for the Evans family and Robin Jackson at Brooklands rebuilding a crashed QA0258 into the single-seater in which George Harvey-Noble in August 1937 broke the Brooklands Class H Outer Circuit Lap record with a speed of 122.4mph, an all-time record for that capacity.

Specification Q-Type

Wheelbase/track	7' 10⅞"/3' 9"
Suspension	leaf springs front and rear
Wheels/tyres	Side-laced Rudge type 2.5" x 18"/4.75"x18"
Brake drum size	12 inch
Engine/power output	746cc/113bhp
Gearbox	4-speed ENV built Wilson pre-selector
Build dates	18th May 1934 to 20th September 1934
Cars built	8

The Zoller supercharger used to boost the power from the 746cc engine to a claimed 113bhp at 7200rpm.

A workmanlike dashboard with a full range of instruments was offered as standard with the Q-types. The pre-selector gearbox is also seen in this picture.

The 19-gallon fuel tank shaped to match the body sat behind the driver, and twin 6-volt batteries were fitted under the lifting tail section.

The R-Type Midget

Although we are all great fans of the MG marque, we have to admit that the cars built between the mid-1930s and the closure of Abingdon in 1980 were never at the cutting edge of technological progress. Their strength and popularity rested almost entirely on their styling and affordability, rather than being of truly innovative design or the ultimate in class-leading performance. Operating always under the constraints imposed by the parent organisation, the MG Car Company remarkably managed to build a whole raft of models that had almost universal appeal. Despite having a budget that would hardly keep the likes of Ford in tea and biscuits for the staff, in the post-war years the small Abingdon team built cars that led the world in export markets.

Having said that most MGs built since the 1930s were based on conventional practice, that was not the case in the early days of the marque, and for a time they even looked set to lead the industry in the search for new and better ways to build racing and sports cars. In 1935 an MG racing car was announced that had a really advanced chassis and a suspension system that promised new standards of road holding. Furthermore, this technology was already earmarked for use in a forthcoming luxury saloon MG. That both projects were to be axed within weeks was a tragedy, both for MG and for the British motor industry as a whole.

In the early years of the marque, along with Cecil Kimber, Hubert Noel Charles was probably the man most responsible for shaping the way the cars developed. This talented designer held a BSc in Engineering from London University and Kimber met him after Charles went to Morris Motors at Cowley as a technical assistant on production. Kimber first employed his talents on a part-time basis to assist in the design and development of the 14/28 and 14/40 models, and close contact during this period led to the two of them becoming firm friends. When MG production moved to Abingdon in 1930 Charles was engaged to run the drawing office and under his direction the effective and long-lived MG chassis first used for EX120 and the C-type was developed.

The string of new models that emerged from Abingdon in the early 1930s, and the growing stature of the marque in national and international motor racing, was due in no small measure to the genius of Charles and the skills and dedication of the small team

The revolutionary R-type rolling chassis with independent suspension on all four wheels.

of men who worked with him. The small-capacity, OHC engines were developed progressively to the stage reached when the 750cc, four-cylinder unit in the 1934 Q-type was producing a greater power output per litre than any other racing engine of its time. This made the car a winner but also highlighted the relative lack of traction and road holding available from the standard MG, leaf spring suspended chassis with its solid front and rear axles.

Current thinking was that stiff, tape-bound leaf springs restrained by friction dampers were the best arrangement for reducing roll and controlling the movement of rigid front and rear axles. Often axle deflection was so restricted that only the flexing of the chassis over bumps kept all four wheels on the ground. This worked efficiently on well-surfaced circuits and gave the cars excellent handing. However, show the car a bump mid-corner and things went wrong very quickly, as many a driver found to their cost.

To better use the considerable power produced by the racing engines it was going to be necessary to devise a way of keeping all four wheels on the ground for as long as possible, whilst coping with the indifferent surfaces found at many race venues, for example the notorious bumps in the Brooklands concrete. Elsewhere, particularly in Europe, designers were turning to forms of independent suspension as way of ensuring that the wheels stayed in contact with the road surface. It was obvious that using solid axles imposed an inherent disadvantage, as the vertical movement of any one wheel would automatically affect the other mounted on the same axle, no matter how firm the suspension. It was relatively easy to fit separate axles for the front wheels, but less so for those at the rear where they also had to do the job of transmitting power to the road surface.

Charles quickly realised that there was little use in merely fitting a form of independent suspension to the existing design of MG chassis. To take full advantage of fitting softer springs to keep the wheels on the road, the chassis had to be far stiffer, in order to provide a rigid mounting for the suspension arms and springs. This is where he was to take a totally different approach, producing a radical departure from previous practice.

Working under the direction of Charles, the design team of Cecil Cousins, Syd Enever and Bill Renwick devised a light and rigid chassis for the new MG racing car, the R-type. This consisted of a central backbone that ran from just behind the driver's seat to the back of the gearbox, where it divided into two separate arms each running to the front on either side of the power unit. A box section united the front legs of the chassis and the differential was attached to the rear of the structure. The immensely strong chassis was electrically welded from 16-gauge steel, but light enough to be carried by one man.

Double wishbones independently suspended by torsion bars replaced the beam axles and leaf springs fitted to previous MGs. The torsion bars provided the springing medium by resisting twisting loads imposed as the wishbones were deflected. They were mounted parallel to the frame, and were adjustable to vary the ride height. Damping was provided by

With the R-type came a special steering box mounted on the firewall that controlled each front wheel separately. The instrument panel was fixed to the bulkhead to allow easy removal of the body panels.

Drive for the Zoller supercharger was taken directly from the front of the engine and this, like the Q-type, produced 113bhp at 7200rpm.

The differential transferred the drive to the rear wheels through two short shafts. Torsion bars provided the springs.

hydraulic shock absorbers; these were later to prove a weak link in the design. Power from the engine was transmitted to the rear by a short prop-shaft via a pre-selector gearbox fitted with a clutch not controlled by the driver. This was inserted to prevent excessive torque from damaging the final drive. A quadrant lever alongside the steering wheel operated the gear selection for the Wilson pre-selector unit; a foot pedal that was like a clutch pedal for a convention gearbox controlled the actual operation of the change.

The chassis-mounted differential transferred power to the rear wheels via two short drive shafts that incorporated sliding splines and universal joints.

Power was provided by a slightly modified version of the already-successful Q-type engine. Efforts were made to improve reliability, necessary with the front-mounted Zoller blower giving induction pressures of around 28lb, and an output of over 110bhp. The central driver's seat was mounted over the transmission tunnel, placing the pedal operating the pre-selector gearbox on the left and throttle and brake pedals on the right. The fuel tank mounted behind the driving seat was shaped to match the external panels. The steering box was specially constructed for the car and featured twin drop arms, one to operate each front wheel. Despite the modernity of the rest of the design, the car retained a cable-operated system for the brakes with the external handbrake working on all four wheels, as was usual MG practice.

The instrument panel was carried on a steel framework fixed to the chassis so that it remained in place once the aluminium panels providing the bodywork were removed. A neat, sloping version of the MG grille was mounted ahead of the radiator and overall the car looked every inch a racer and quite unlike anything else previously built by the company.

The plan was to assemble an initial batch of ten cars and these were completed between April and June 1935. There was every hope that more would be needed and that the advanced chassis technology would soon appear in the big MG saloon, a prototype of which was already at an advanced stage of development. However, this was not to be and further development of the new racing car was stilled soon after the car was launched by the announcement of a radical reorganisation of the company. The changes that followed from this were to alter the future direction of the MG marque and terminate their participation at the leading edge of technology, occasional record-breaking attempts and competition participation apart.

As a result of an appraisal of all of his various businesses, and in line with the thinking of Leonard Lord who had been appointed Managing Director of Morris Motors a year or so earlier, on the 1st July 1935 William Morris sold MG to Morris Motors. The effect of this was to bring the company under the overall control of Lord, who is said not to have liked Kimber, or anyone else with talent. Having seen the racing department at Abingdon and the furious activity building the new R-type, he ordered it to be closed and for the design and development work on future models to move to Cowley. Charles went there and continued to work on MG projects, but these

Wal Handley drove an R-type in the 1935 Mannin Beg race on the Isle of Man as part of a three car team entered by George Eyston, who drove one car with Norman Black in the other.

RA0257 photographed after restoration by Gerhard Maier. Post rebuild the car was at the MG Car Club Silverstone meeting in 1999 where it was reunited with its first owner, Ian Connell.

were based around conventional components from other vehicles in the Nuffield Group and did not break any new ground.

So to return to the R-types that were built, how successful were they? Immediately following their public announcement six were entered for a JCC International Trophy Race held at Brooklands on 6th May. Chassis RA0251, RA0252 and RA0253 were run as a semi-official factory team under the control of George Eyston, the drivers being Norman Black, Wal Handley and George, Doreen Evans was at the wheel of RA0255, which had been purchased by the family firm, Bellevue Garage. W. Esplen, the first owner, entered RA0256 and shared the driving with Gunnar Poppe. W.G. Everitt and Sir Malcolm Campbell shared RA0260. In the race the cars ran well over the bumpy track but exhibited an alarming amount of roll on the corners. As a brand new design teething troubles were inevitable and just two of the cars completed the gruelling race. The Campbell/Everitt car was sixth overall and first in class and Doreen Evans came home in seventh place and second in class.

The revolutionary design was certainly not without its defects and the cars proved to have too high a roll centre and their torsion bars did not have exactly the right torsional stiffness. As a result the lean on corners was rather disconcerting and the rear end tended to have more of a tendency to break away than should have been the case. Additionally, the shock absorber technology of the time was not well adapted to coping with relatively long-travel suspensions and the units overheated and become less effective as races progressed. None of those shortcomings would have hampered progress for long, given the full attention of

Rear suspension of RA0257.

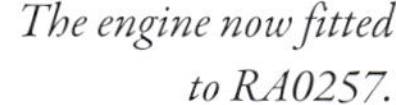

The engine now fitted to RA0257.

the development department, but that was no longer an option now that it had been transferred to Cowley. So, without any improvements forthcoming from the factory, the future of the R-type rested with the private owners.

Doreen Evans continued to campaign her car and at Shelsley Walsh on 18th May set a new ladies' record for the hill. As we have seen, George Eyston had entered a team of three cars for the first meeting, where their results had been rather disappointing, and on 20th May the team fared little better when they all had to retire from the Mannin Beg Race on the Isle of Man. However, Bobby Baird upheld R-type honours by taking fourth place in his car. For the British Empire Trophy race at Brooklands on 6th July Eyston again entered three R-types, driven by himself, Handley and Black. Handley was unclassified, Black finished in fifth place and Eyston was placed fourteenth after a troubled run. Following the withdrawal of factory support, Eyston must have decided not to continue running the R-types and his three cars were put up for sale. One of them was eventually owned and run by Kenneth Evans.

Despite their revolutionary design, the R-type was destined for a comparatively short career at the top level of motor sport. The reasons for this are not hard to find. In the 1500cc class for international events a 750cc car was at a severe disadvantage and in the 750cc class at national meetings MGs dominance was in serious jeopardy once the Murray Jamieson designed Austin twin-cam racing cars arrived in 1936. These were lighter than the R-types and their Roots-blown engines would safely run to 9000rpm, giving the cars 125mph performance. Although the chassis lacked the sophistication of the R-type, it had solid axles with a transverse leaf spring at the front and quarter-elliptic rear springs, the low build and light weight gave it superior road-holding on relatively smooth tracks. Although the factory team cars in the hands of Dodson and Handley only raced in British events, they were very successful.

Perhaps the most interesting development carried out in an effort to improve the performance of the R-type for the 1936 season was the fitting to three of the cars of twin overhead camshaft cylinder heads. These heads were developed by Pomeroy and McEvoy and were installed in the ex-Eyston car run by Bellevue Garage for Kenneth Evans, and to the cars raced by Ian Connell and Douglas Briault. The first race for the twin-cam cars was the British Empire Trophy Race at Donington on 4th April 1936. Disappointingly, all three cars failed to finish and whilst running did not exhibit quite the expected improvement in performance. Future races did reveal some of the potential of the special cylinder heads, but there were also a number of reliability problems.

With hindsight it is easy to see that with the R-type and the proposed new saloon the company were taking the first tentative steps towards building cars that possessed the handling, ride and road holding characteristics we now have come to expect. However, there was still a way to go and at a time when sales, and thus profits, were not strong one can quite easily see why Lord decided to curtail the pioneering efforts in order to concentrate on making conventional vehicles, which he hoped would be more profitable.

Luckily, of the very few cars built, it would seem that only one cannot now be traced, although the survivors are not all in complete, running order. In recent years we have even seen some of the cars entered at MG meetings.

Specification R-Type

Wheelbase/track	7' 6½"/Front 3' 10⅜ Rear 3' 9½"
Suspension	Independent front and rear by wishbones and torsion bars
Wheels/tyres	Side laced wire, Rudge type, 3.00" x 18"/4.75"x18"
Brake drum size	12 inch
Engine/power output	746cc/113bhp
Gearbox	4-speed ENV built Wilson pre-selector
Build dates	29th April 1935 to 6th May 1935
Cars built	10

The TA & TB Midgets

By 1935, when Lord Nuffield sold the MG Car Company to the Nuffield Group and the responsibility for the design of new models passed to Cowley, the reputation of the marque had been established on the back of competition successes. When they had moved in 1930 to Abingdon the only models produced were the 18/80 six-cylinder cars and the M-type Midget. By 1935 they had built a wide range of sports and racing cars capable of taking on and beating all others in their class. On the other hand, although some models had sold in profitable volumes, others struggled to find sufficient customers and probably did nothing to improve the company balance sheet.

The transfer of ownership has been blamed for forcing the company to cease its racing activities and to rationalise the production models. No doubt the change of control was partly to blame, but even had the sale not gone ahead the final outcome would have probably been little different. Sir William Morris, who had become Lord Nuffield in 1934, was not himself a fan of racing and was keen that if his products were raced that they should be seen to be similar to cars that could be bought by the customer. Although there has been much debate as to whether their racing activities made or lost money for the company, there is no doubt that their products were becoming more and more specialised and required different components to those used for other cars built by the group. The R-type racing car featured earlier is a prime example. It is likely, therefore, that even if the company had remained under Lord Nuffield's direct control changes may have happened anyway.

The move of the design and development offices

Two variants of the adverts run at the TA's launch.

First full TA catalogue.

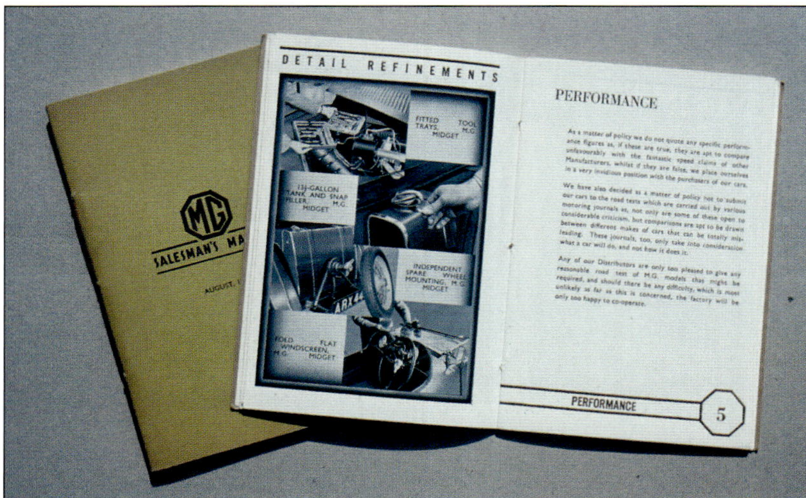

Booklets produced for the salesmen in the showroom to help them sell the TA Midget.

Detail from later TA catalogue.

from Abingdon to Cowley, where they were to remain until work on the development of the MGA began, had an immediate effect. This was not always a benefit as development of new models was sometimes a lot slower than it had been under the small team at Abingdon. The replacements for the six-cylinder Magnas and Magnettes were VA and SA saloons and tourers that turned out to be up-market and stylish cars with components from Morris and Wolseley parts bins. These cars had considerable showroom appeal but were more suited to everyday use than competition work. Truthfully, the same could also have been said of most of the tourer and saloon versions of the previous models.

The final OHC version of the popular Midget offered for sale was the PB. This had an engine with a slightly larger capacity than the previous four-cylinder cars, but in standard tune it still needed to be worked fairly hard to achieve good performance. The last PB Midget rolled off the Abingdon production line in February 1936, but there were obviously quite a few examples still in the hands of dealers during the early months of that year. Cars were still being lent to the press and *The Autocar* published a full road test in January, as did *Motor Sport* in April, and neither mentioned that the model was at the end of its life.

The relatively slow development process for a replacement Midget meant that the first public announcement of a new model appeared some four months after the last PB left the line. In June the major car magazines all carried detailed descriptions of the new Midget. The prototype TA, chassis number 0251, had been built in early March and chassis 0252 four weeks later. Volume production was underway by the end of June, just about in time for some examples to go out to the dealers to meet any demand stimulated by the magazine articles.

Those magazine reports of the new T Series Midget all stressed its larger size than the PB and consequent improvement in space for occupants and luggage. However, basically the design followed a pattern established once the company had developed their own chassis for EX120 and then used this for the C-type, D-type and subsequent models. For the TA the frame was strengthened by boxing-in the front of the side frames, but the system locating the rear end of the leaf springs in bronze trunnion bushes was retained.

Hydraulic brakes were beginning to become universally adopted by the motor industry so this system was used for the new car. Drivers at the time must have welcomed the change although, aesthetically, the smaller drums fitted to the new car did not look quite as impressive as the large twelve-inch ones used for the previous P-type Midgets. The handbrake design

Studio pictures of the first TA fitted with narrow rear wings and 15-gallon fuel tank. On this first TA the dashboard had the reading and 30mph lamps outboard of the instruments, rather than either side of the central panel.

was similar to that fitted to the earlier cars but now only worked the rear wheels, rather than all four.

Although the team at Abingdon had developed the Wolseley-derived OHC engines to the point where they were producing higher power outputs per litre than almost any other engines in production, these were not by then fitted to any other Nuffield products. For the group as a whole this made no sense, so for the TA the design team at Cowley turned to the OHV engine destined for the Wolseley 10/40 and Morris Ten. This unit in MG form was designated the MPJG and given camshaft and manifold changes, plus twin SU carburettors, to increase the power to 50bhp. The

This factory picture of an early TA shows the narrow rear wings.

TA with wider rear wings used by The Motor *magazine for their road test article.*

A picture showing how the hood should be folded, possibly intended for use in a handbook.

final version of the four-cylinder OHC engine, used for the PB, produced 43bhp at 5500rpm from its 939cc, whereas the 1292cc, TA engine produced maximum power at only 4200rpm. This, then, was the essential difference between the two engines. One was a high-revving and very sporting unit capable of producing a good power output for its capacity, whereas the other was rather less free-revving but was capable of good performance and gave improved torque at lower engine speeds. However, the TA engine was both larger and much heavier than the earlier OHC unit.

To improve refinement, the new engine was provided with rubber mountings and the radiator was now fixed directly to the chassis. The four-speed gearbox gained synchromesh on the upper ratios and was driven from the engine via a cork-faced clutch running in oil. This system was very popular at the time as it was thought to give a smooth feel to the clutch. The body followed

A studio picture of the same, later TA.

the style that had been established for MG two-seaters when the J2 arrived in 1932. These ash-framed bodies were built at Morris Bodies Branch, not Carbodies, and provided more generous room for both driver and passenger than had been available to owners of the earlier cars. In particular there was now considerably more room behind the bench-style seats for a reasonable amount of luggage for touring holidays, as well as a separate compartment in which to stow the side-screens. The MG sports car was becoming a much more serious form of everyday transport.

The engine bay of a restored TA showing the inlet manifold and the air cleaner fitted to the Morris-derived power unit.

With an engine capacity a little bit larger than the last of the six-cylinder Magnettes, and now the only two-seater sports car available from Abingdon, the T Series Midget had to be good enough to appeal to both the owners of the earlier MG Midgets and to those who would have previously bought the rather more expensive two-seater Magnas and Magnettes. Judged by contemporary press reports, buyers welcomed the new car and were happy with the rather fewer demands made upon their skills to extract a similar performance from them than had been required with earlier models.

The first road tests to appear in the motoring press stressed that, although there had been a great many changes, the essential character of the car was unaltered. They said that it had exceptionally good performance for a car of that engine capacity and that its handling was vastly better than that offered by the average touring cars of the period. They remarked upon the appearance of greater solidity given by the longer wheelbase, wider track, bigger body and longer bonnet. On the road they said that the car had a different feel, softer, quieter and with a power unit that was far more flexible at low engine speeds. In short, the new model was altogether easier to drive.

The performance figures they recorded, 23.1 seconds to 60mph and maximum of 77mph, compared well with those for the previous model, the PB, which were 27 seconds to 60mph and a maximum of 71mph; albeit these were recorded under adverse conditions. Tests in some magazines gave even better figures for the new car;

The TA engine and gearbox.

The owner of this restored TA retained the original power unit and cork clutch and in using his car was happy with them.

Optional luggage racks would fit the TA, TB or TC models.

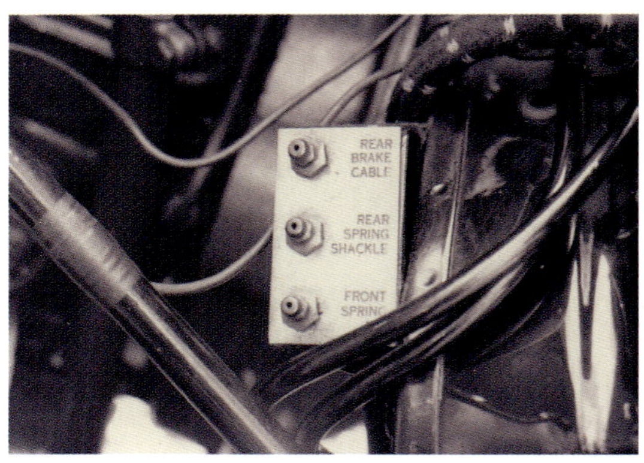

The grouped nipples for oiling the suspension fitted to the later TAs and all TB models.

The easiest way to quickly distinguish a TA or TB from the later TC is by the number of rubber strips on the running boards. The TA & TB have three on each, the TC only two.

one quoting a top speed as high as 80mph. Although the Midget had grown up quite a lot it still seemed to appeal to the same sorts of customers and many part-exchanged their older models for the new car. The price of the T Series Midget was £222, the same as that charged for the PB, so this was in its favour, and those deserting the ranks of six-cylinder MG owners to buy the Midget were actually purchasing a cheaper car, but one of similar size and performance.

For the 1939 model year the company modified and improved the car by fitting a version of the engine developed for the then new Morris 10. This engine, in MG form known as the XPAG, was later to earn a considerable reputation as being capable of being tuned to give high outputs. Indeed, in the early 1950s the builders of some small competition specials and racing cars successfully used tuned versions of this engine. This new version of the T Series was known as the TB, although the Second World War was to call a halt to production of the revised model after only a few hundred had been built. In recent years a great many of the surviving TAs have been converted to TB specification by installing XPAG power units in various states of tune.

So, how do we assess the merits of the TA? The poor reputation of what was, even in the late 1930s, a power unit looking a bit dated is partly because in recent years many have developed cracked cylinder heads or porous blocks. Casting techniques in the 1930s were not as well developed as they are now and blocks, especially ones that have been bored, often fail to keep oil and water apart, but modern injection techniques developed for use on aluminium castings can overcome the problem. The engine is not as powerful as the XPAG unit, or as able to be tuned to produce extra bhp, but on the other hand, it has plenty of torque and gives a smooth power delivery. The TA has many of the virtues of the later T-types, with the added bonus of being a pre-war model and comparatively rare. The remaining genuine TB models are even less available and consequently more expensive. They possess most of the virtues of the later TC, as well as being a pre-war model and therefore eligible to run in events not open to the later T-types.

This TA was sold originally to the Lancashire Constabulary, when it would have been finished in this colour scheme of black with blue leather seats.

TA Changes In Production

Mechanical

From engine number MPJG/684 the gearbox fitted with synchromesh on third and top gears.

TA 0652	Engine breather pipe modified.
TA 0824	Petrol tap and pipe modified.
MPJG/1018	Water pump fitted with oil cup in place of greaser.
MPJG/1139	Oil filter changed.
MPJG/1294	Clutch cover plate modified.
MPJG/1514	Oil filter changed again.
TA 1306	Handbrake cross shaft fitted with return spring to improve the fly off action.
MPJG/1605	Double valve springs replaced by triple.
TA 1877	Carburettor linkage modified.
TA 1990	Slow running control modified and fitted with a return spring.
TA 2232	A flexible section was added to oil pressure gauge line.
TA 2253	The chassis lubrication was modified and a grouped nipple system fitted.
TA 2254	Front springs modified.
MPJG/2622	Oil deflecting plate fitted to front of camshaft.
MPJG/2847	Valve spring caps modified.
MPJG/3053	Rocker shaft supports modified.
TA2882	Steering column made adjustable and steering box ratio changed.

The TB engine and gearbox. This air cleaner arrangement was continued for the TC.

Other Changes

TA 1250 At about this point the body style changed. The rear wings were widened and the petrol tank width reduced. The earlier TAs are usually now referred to as narrow wing cars.

TA 1770 Wheels changed from side laced to centre laced. Sometime during the first year of production a rubber cover replaced the carpet over the gearbox.

TB Changes In Production

Mechanical

TB 0307	Crankshaft pulley modified.
XPAG/645	Tappet cover modified.

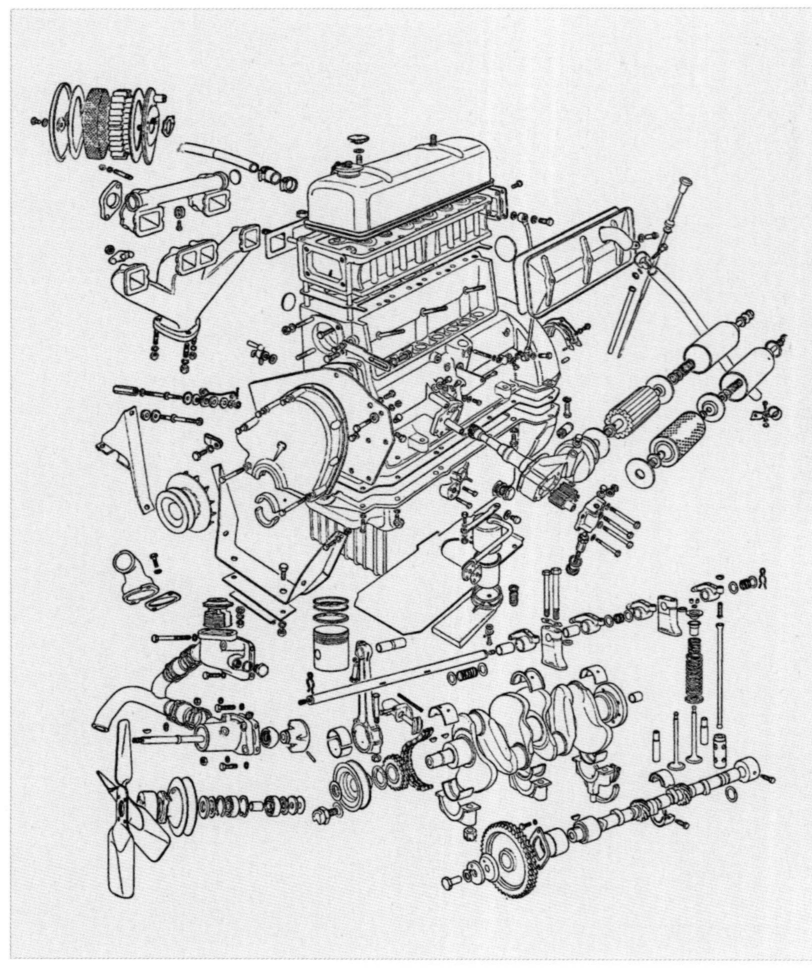

Engine exploded. The XPAG type power unit fitted to all Midgets from the TB onwards. There are many detail differences between models, air cleaners for example.

A TB probably photographed in one of the villages near Abingdon.

The TA & TB In Competition

The factory abandoned the racing programme in 1935. The TA was hardly suitable for this purpose anyway, but they did maintain their support of the Cream Cracker and the Musketeers trials teams, who brought success and much needed publicity to the marque. When the new car was announced it became obvious that these teams would have to move over to using the T Series if the company were to continue to derive any sales benefit from the efforts of the trials drivers.

For the Cream Cracker team three TAs were modified for use in trials and at the same time three TAs were also built for the Musketeer team. The six TAs went down the line in December 1936 with chassis numbers 930, 932 and 934 prepared for the Cream Cracker drivers, and 931, 933 and 935 for the Musketeer team. The Cream Cracker cars were finished in cream with brown wings, like the previous Musketeer cars, but those destined for that team were painted red.

Each car was sold to its regular driver and it was set out that the price included a set of 19-inch wheels fitted with 4.50 competition tyres on the front and standard 4.50 tyres for the rear. In addition there were two 16-inch wheels with 6.00 competition tyres to go on the rear when tackling the timed sections of a trial. The drivers were also given a further five tyres, the sizes at their choice. All the tyres could be replaced during the year free of charge provided the old ones were returned.

Every car came with a spare differential, a set of half-shafts, four valve rockers and two pushrods, a set of valve springs and a spare inner tube. A new set of spark plugs was supplied for each event. Each driver was given an amount of credit to cover maintenance at Abingdon, to be carried out in what was stipulated to be as economical a manner as possible. Any parts needed over and above breakages also had to come out of this allowance. A large increase in power had previously been obtained by supercharging the OHC engines, but at the time it was not considered wise to go that route with the OHV Morris unit. Instead, attention turned

All the 1937 Cream Cracker team cars and drivers during the Torquay Rally.

to weight reduction. Aluminium bonnets and valances, together with aluminium door skins, saved quite a few pounds, as did cycle wings in place of the attractive but heavy swept ones fitted to the TA. At the front, lengthened J2 stays held the wings well above the tyres, aided by different road springs to raise ride height. A special bracket to carry twin spare wheels was fitted to the rear of the chassis.

Work on the engine consisted of removing metal from the cylinder head to raise compression, plus the necessary alterations to the valve gear to compensate. Stronger valve springs, cotters and bottom collars were fitted to the head after the combustion chambers had been reshaped and polished. The twin SU carburettors were given different needles and the end result was an engine capable of producing a useful amount more than the standard 50bhp. A holder to contain six spare spark plugs was fitted to the bulkhead. Oil and water temperature gauges were added to the standard instrumentation. A hand throttle operated by a Bowden cable was fitted to help the driver maintain power when rough going could make keeping steady pressure on the throttle pedal difficult.

Trials usually involved negotiating rough, rocky tracks and as the TA had hydraulic, rather than cable-operated brakes, these needed to be protected from damage. The brake pipes were armoured and re-routed and the single master cylinder was replaced with a double, shielded from damage by a steel plate. The exhaust pipe and silencer were moved to make them less vulnerable. The differential had the same final drive ratio, but to improve hill-climbing ability first, second and third gears were lower. The oil filter was raised out of harm's way and after the first event pressed steel sumps replaced the standard aluminium ones.

An article concerning the modification made to TA trials cars published in *The Sports Car*, a magazine sent to all MG Car Club members and supported by the MG Car Company, mentioned

1938 Cream Cracker TAs, BBL 78 Toulmin and BBL 79 Crawford. By this time the cars were fitted with a VA engine bored out to 1708cc.

A.G. Imhof's Cream Cracker TA with its spare wheel mounting in front of the radiator. He felt that being able to adjust weight balance by moving the wheel from back to front of the car gave him an advantage on certain tests.

The ex-Cream Cracker TA on the Nailsworth Ladder during 1995 reunion for all the surviving works trials team cars.

Ken Selby piloting ABL 964 up the Nailsworth Ladder in the 1995 reunion.

that the factory were willing to carry out similar alterations for any owners wishing to use their TAs in such events. But prices were not mentioned. At that stage it was still being recommended that the engine should not be supercharged, but letters printed in the magazine reveal that some did decide to try this route.

A list giving possible events to be entered in 1937 was given to the drivers, who had some leeway as to which they chose, but they were asked to enter at least a dozen. The list eventually produced covered an ambitious eighteen-event programme. Although the drivers had to buy their cars from the factory this was at a very advantageous price well below the actual cost. They could also sell them back at the end of the year. For example, the cars supplied the following year cost £210 and had a fixed buy-back price of £170.

The first outing for the TA Cream Cracker cars was the Exeter Trial, which started on New Year's Day 1937. They had yet to receive their cream and brown paint and there were temporary signs on the bonnets to identify the team. The drivers of the TAs were team leader, Maurice Toulmin in ABL 960, Kenneth Crawford in ABL 962 and J.E.S. 'Jesus' Jones in ABL 964. The Musketeers still ran the very potent L/N Magnette specials. Both teams earned a clean sheet of Premier Awards and the Musketeers took the Team Award.

The ex-Cream Cracker TA photographed in recent years when owned and used in competition by Andy King.

After the Exeter the cars went back to Abingdon to be finished off before their next outing. Small niggles were corrected and alterations made where strenuous use proved these necessary. There then followed a full season of events, during which the TA Cream Cracker cars scored a number of successes.

The final event for the 1937 TAs in the hands of the Cream Cracker drivers was the Exeter Trial in January 1938, their new TAs, now fitted with the 1548cc VA engines, not being ready in time. By then the capacity of these engines had been increased to 1708cc by overboring and fitting WA pistons. The cars were sold off after the Exeter, probably that year to their drivers who could make a profit disposing of them privately, hence a ruling for the 1938 cars that they must be sold back to the factory.

Like the other MG team, the Musketeers had changed over to TAs for 1937, running ABL 961, ABL 963 and ABL 965 to the same specification as that used for the Cream Cracker cars. Likewise for 1938 new cars, BBL 82, BBL 83 and BBL 84 replaced these. In addition, BJB 412 was provided for new team member Dickie Green. However this last series of team cars differed from the Cream Crackers as they were fitted with their modified TA engines running with Laystall crankshafts and Marshall 110 superchargers. All these Musketeer cars were painted red, rather than cream and brown.

Red painted Musketeer TA, ABL 965 Aramis on the Welsh Rally in 1937.

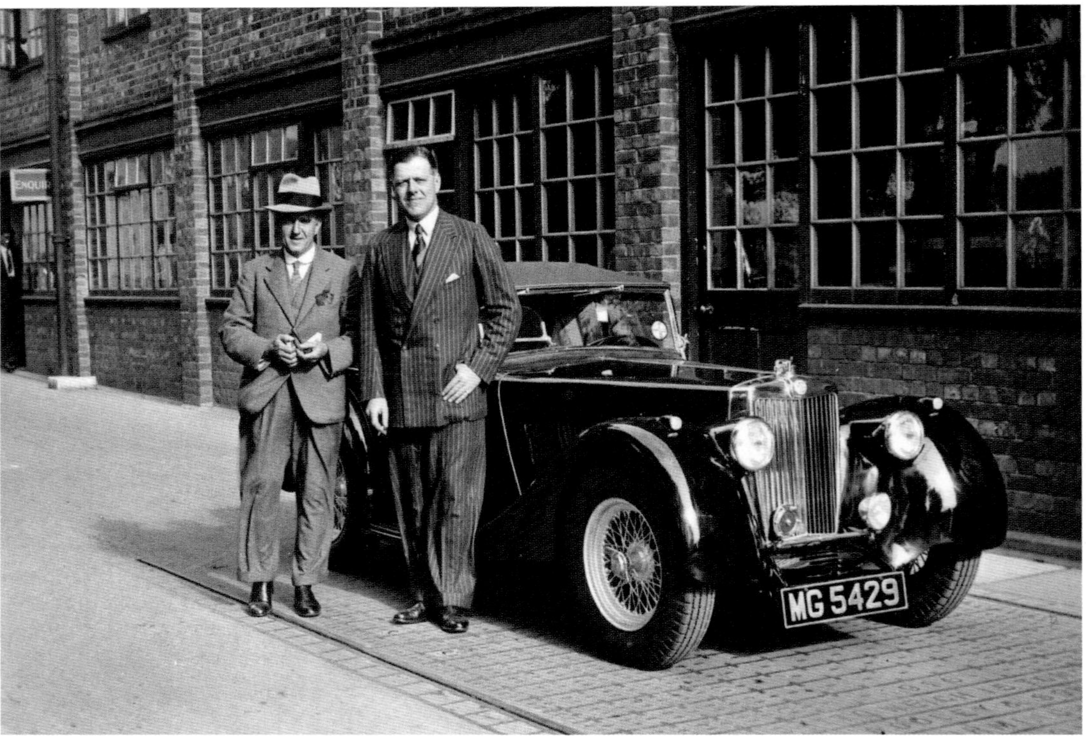

The only TA fitted with a special body that is well documented is the car here being handed over to the owner, Lord Ashby, by Cecil Kimber.

TA/TB Special Bodied Cars

Unlike the earlier Midgets, very few TAs are documented as having been built originally with special bodies, although 10 were sold as rolling chassis with possibly some going abroad to be fitted there with locally made bodies. University Motors took one rolling chassis and had one of their DHC bodies fitted to this, but there are no records to show if this was a two- or four-seater. The TA built for Lord Ashby and photographed being handed over to him by Cecil Kimber was marked as a special in the surviving book that listed the number of the engine fitted to each TA chassis. As it appeared to have had a standard TA body tub, this might indicate that the car left Abingdon just minus some parts, for example wings and headlamps, for fitting by the coachbuilder, rather than being sold as a rolling chassis. Monaco Motors took one TB rolling chassis, fitting this with a lightweight body for the 1939 Tourist Trophy, which was then cancelled when war on Germany was declared.

TA & TB Tickford

Given the British climate, there are many occasions when even the really keen sports car enthusiasts yearn for some protection from the weather. The folding hoods and removable side screens provided by most manufacturers in the heyday of the British sports car did give some shelter from the elements, but this fell far below that offered by even the most modest saloon. What was really needed was a hood that gave as much comfort and protection in poor weather as a fixed roof, whilst retaining all the advantages and pleasures of an open sports car when the sun shone.

Salmons & Sons, coachbuilders of Newport Pagnell, were founded in 1820 and the Salmons family ran the company right up to 1939. They survived the change from building horse-drawn vehicles to motorcars and weathered the lean years of the depression that saw many of their competitors into bankruptcy. Always innovators, they made their first car body as early as 1898 and were exponents of all-weather bodywork. The first Tickford drophead saloon was announced in 1925 and the unique feature of this was a geared mechanism that allowed the owner to lower the hood by inserting a handle and winding it down. Their use of the term saloon was borne of a desire to emphasise the virtues of closed-car comfort in an open car. This style of coachwork became their main business and they even offered a service adapting a saloon car to incorporate a folding roof; the side windows were usually retained.

At a time when fewer customers were having their cars coachbuilt, Salmons managed to survive by gaining orders direct from the car companies so that their style of bodies could be offered as part of the manufacturer's

One of the first production TAs with a Tickford body photographed in the Cowley studio.

standard range. Vauxhall, Rover, Hillman and Talbot were all sold with Tickford bodies, and in time a refinement of the design saw the three-position head introduced. This meant that the car could be used closed, fully open, or with just the section above the front seats rolled back so that the rear panel provided some protection from the elements.

There is evidence that Salmons converted at least one MG in the early 1930s as the company placed advertisements for a Tickford foursome coupé on a Midget chassis in 1933, 1934 and 1935. These could have related to more than one example as in one advertisement the car was described as a 1931 model, thus an M- or D-type, and in another as a 1933/34 model. The latter would most likely have been on a J1 chassis. There was also an advertisement for a Tickford drophead pillarless coupé, which was described as being on a KD chassis. This could have been one of the company's folding roof conversions of a KN pillarless saloon, but no other details of the car survive.

In 1937 volume production of Tickford bodies for The MG Car Company commenced. This came with the announcement of the drophead coupé versions of the recently introduced 2-litre SA and 1 1/2-litre VA models; these to be sold by dealers alongside those completed at Abingdon as standard production cars. The Tickford drophead coupés were immediately popular with buyers and were certainly the most attractive models in the range.

The TA was launched in 1936 as a replacement for the two-seater sports models previously built by MG. Initially the TA was only produced as an open two-

The cockpit of one of the first Tickford TAs.

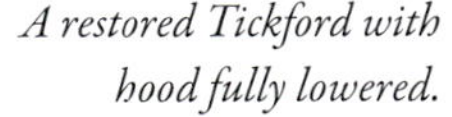

A restored Tickford with hood fully lowered.

The two shades of blue colour scheme was one of the standard options with the TA Tickford.

seater, except for one airline coupé that was probably assembled merely as a way of using up a remaining body once production of the OHC cars ceased, although one source says that the TA Airline body was larger than those fitted to the OHC cars and that two were built. However, following the success of the Tickford versions of other models of MG, in 1938 a TA with the Tickford three-position top was announced.

TA Tickford dashboard and interior with separate bucket seats.

Complete assembly of the standard cars at Abingdon used bodies that arrived at the factory already painted and trimmed. The Tickford MGs, however, were built up to running chassis stage and then driven the 45 miles to Newport Pagnell to have the bodies fitted. For the journey the chassis were given easily removed rudimentary bodywork consisting of wings that just about complied with the road traffic laws, and a seat with little protection for the hapless driver. The removed temporary bodies were then transported back to Abingdon.

At Newport Pagnell the Tickford bodywork started life as a pile of ash sections that had been shaped in the mill, using a number of complicated formers to ensure that each piece would fit accurately. These timber sections were then united in a body jig fitted with clamps that held each piece of wood in exactly the right place. Assembling the body in this fashion ensured that the rest of the parts - doors, outer skinning, windscreen, etc. would fit without adjustment. The coachbuilders were well equipped and there was even a foundry within the factory that made the many special fittings used on the cars, like the distinctive pram-irons. They did their own chrome plating, as well as the more traditional jobs like polishing the veneers for the dashboard and trimming the seats. Overall there were around 500 people on the payroll, almost as many as were employed at Abingdon at the time.

A TA Tickford is suited to use for driving on country lanes and by-roads. It is a bit low-geared for motorway driving.

The rear window in the hood is small so an outside mirror is essential.

The Tickford coupés were available in a wider choice of colours than the standard cars and, in addition to having better protection from the weather, they were fitted with separate bucket seats, a fully carpeted interior, semaphore-style direction indicators, an ashtray and an interior light just above the small glass rear window. The windscreen wiper motor was no longer mounted on the top of the windscreen frame, but instead was installed beneath the bonnet, and the dashboard was altered from that used on the standard cars. All in all, the TA Tickford was a quality car and the type of people who bought them tended not to be looking so much for sports car performance as for a comfortable touring two-seater, and the space available behind the seats was sufficient to hold a reasonable amount of luggage. However, a few Tickford TAs were used in club competitions, although their greater weight did impose a small performance penalty.

The greater bulk of the lowered hood restricted rearward visibility, but the higher doors reduced wind buffeting for the occupants, and when the substantial soft top was raised this made the interior of the car quieter. For its time, the TA Tickford was an extremely attractive small car, and when in 1939 the XPAG engine became available with the introduction of the TB this gave the car even better performance. Talking figures, a look at a contemporary appraisal of a TA

With only the section above the seats open the occupants are still given some protection from the elements.

A restored TA Tickford.

1939 brochure for the TB Tickford.

Specification TA/TB

Wheelbase/track	7' 10"/3'9"
Suspension	Leaf springs front and rear
Wheels/tyres	Rudge type 2.50" x 19"/4.50"x19"
Brake drum size	9 inch
Engine/power output	TA 1292cc/50bhp
	TB 1250cc/54bhp
Gearbox	TA 4-speed, with synchromesh on third and top
	TB 4-speed, synchromesh on top three ratios
Build dates	TA 25th June 1936 to 17th April 1939
	TB 11th May 1939 to Early October 1939
Cars built	TA/TB
	Open sports TA 2740/TB 322
	Airline Coupé TA 1
	Tickford Coupé TA 252/TB 57
	Chassis TA 10

Tickford reveals that the top speed was in the order of 75/80mph and that the extra weight, around 200lbs, must have blunted acceleration times a little, but did not spoil the journalists' enjoyment of the car. A magazine report written about the TB Tickford in September 1939 heaped lavish praise on the MG and the writers particularly liked the new engine. They found it had improved the performance and was much smoother than the superseded long-stroke TA unit. Of the 359 TBs built around 57 were fitted with Tickford bodies.

The TC Midget

Looking back to a small factory at Abingdon had been employed for the past six years producing tanks for the army, aircraft parts and even complete cockpit fuselage sections for the Albemarle bomber. Members of the pre-war work force who had not been called up to join the forces had been augmented by women recruited from both the local area and from other parts of the country. These largely unskilled people had learned to work to the demanding standard necessary to assemble complex aircraft components, and the production line techniques utilised pre-war to assemble Midgets and Magnettes had proved useful when trying to keep up with the demands of a country fighting for its very existence.

When car production ceased after war was declared in September 1939, the last few MG two-seaters produced had been TB Midgets. These were a development of the TA, which had been in production since 1936 with over 3000 examples built and sold. With the coming of peace in Europe in May1945 the military work began to dry up and it was imperative that the factory return as quickly as possible to making cars. Even whilst the last of the military contracts was being completed, a corner of the factory was turned over to producing Abingdon's first post-war car, the TC Midget.

On the TB, sliding trunnions were used to locate the rear ends of the four half-elliptic leaf springs. These were pivoted at the front end and mounted into bronze trunnions at the rear, which was a system said to provide good lateral location to the springs. In spite of this advantage, when the TC was designed it was decided to change to more conventional rubber-bushed shackles to locate the rear of the springs. These eliminated the problems encountered when the sliding trunnions were insufficiently lubricated. This was now particularly important because it was anticipated that many more cars were to be exported to countries where owners expected them to cover high mileages without much attention.

As with most MGs, the engines for the TA and TB were based on units used in cars produced in other parts of the Nuffield Group. When the TB was introduced the engine designed for the new 1,100cc Series M Morris 10

First TC catalogue was an adaptation of the one issued pre-war for the TB.

Advertisement placed in 1946 for the TC, despite there being virtually no cars available for the home market.

TC rear axle and springs showing the replacement of the TB sliding trunnions with shackles.

was specified. For the MG the bore was increased to 66.5mm to give a capacity of 1250cc. In later years the engine was to prove to be strong enough to cope with considerably greater power output than the 54.4bhp originally produced. In 1945 this engine was specified for the TC with only minor modifications to the oil filter and with the addition of a timing chain tensioner to reduce noise from that area.

The steel-panelled ash-frame body fitted to the TA and TB was retained for the TC, although widened by about four inches at the rear door pillar to give more elbowroom. This change produced one of the easiest ways to identify a TA or TB from a TC as the running boards were reduced in width and had only two tread strips, rather than the three fitted to the earlier cars.

So there in 1945 you had the latest from Abingdon. The chassis design dated from 1931, the general body shape and styling from 1936 and the engine from 1938. Even before the war the MG Midget appeared old fashioned when compared with, for example, the 328 BMW with its more up-to-date bodywork, independent suspension, stiffer chassis and flexible springing. However, in 1945 the choice of available new cars, especially sports cars, was very limited and it isn't surprising that enthusiasts queued up to put their names on the waiting lists for the new TC Midget.

Shortages of raw materials in post-war Britain, and

An early TC rolling chassis with a light grey bulkhead. One change made when the TB was redesigned to create the TC was to move the battery under the bonnet instead of beneath the shelf behind the seats. The space behind the battery box was used to house a very useful tool locker.

the desperate need for foreign exchange, led the newly elected Labour government to impose restrictions on steel supplies. This meant that manufacturers could only build cars if they could obtain supplies of steel, and priority was given to those producing at least three-quarters of their output for export. Actually a higher proportion of the TC production stayed in this country when compared to the later TD, of which a greater percentage was exported. However, demand outstripped the numbers supplied to dealers and it is interesting to see that, such was the post-war demand for sports cars, even quite tired pre-war TAs for a while fetched almost as much as a new TC.

Once the military work ceased, the factory was stripped of all the jigs and fixtures installed to build the complicated weapons of war. The production lines were rebuilt and production of the TC started in earnest. The original 1939 workforce, many of whom had been called up for military service for the duration of the war, returned to take up their old jobs and the majority of the females employed for war work were dismissed. However, particularly after YA saloon production started in 1947, there were still quite a number of female workers employed on the top deck to trim the painted bodies prior to being lowered down to the assembly line.

According to factory records, in 1945 100 TCs were built. These appear to have been laid down in batches and some sources give the total completed as only 81 cars. No matter which figure is correct, at least the factory was back in business, and by December 1945 they had produced a full catalogue for the TC, advertising the car at a price of £375 ex-works plus purchase tax. The catalogue used much of the artwork from the TA and TB catalogues but the shortages of materials and the difficulties of production reduced the choice of colours for the new model to just Black. However, buyers had the chance to select Vellum Beige, Shires Green or Regency Red upholstery. The hood and side-screens were made of tan cloth and the half tonneau of a black waterproof material. Quite a number of TCs produced in 1945 and 1946 seem to have had black hoods and side-screens instead of tan, but just how many isn't recorded.

Actually the December 1945 TC catalogue wasn't the first one issued for the car. As early as April that year the 1939 TB brochure had been reprinted as a series

TC veneered wooden dashboard with flat-faced speedometer and tachometer.

A TC on test prior to delivery.

An early TC engine bay with light grey bulkhead.

TC preliminary announcement. At that stage all the photographs and most of the details were those for the TB but prices, colour schemes, etc., had been omitted. A copy of this publication accompanied a standard letter sent out in response to enquiries from the public about post war-production and referred the inquirers to their nearest distributor.

The factory lost no time in letting members of the press try the new car and in October 1945 *The Autocar* had tried one of them on a number of the more challenging hills used in production car trials. In the 1930s these trials were an extremely important branch of motor sport. The MG Car Company used successes in these by the factory-supported Cream Cracker and Musketeer teams to promote the sale of production MG cars. For example, the catalogue for the TC pictured the three-car team of TAs and billed these as 'the most successful trials cars'.

The Autocar journalist was very impressed with the TC as it climbed all the hills he tried with great ease. He summarised the improvements over the previous model, making much of the wider cockpit and seats and the repositioning of the battery from behind the seats to a more convenient place under the bonnet. The modified spring mountings and new shock absorbers were felt to have improved comfort without sacrificing roadholding. He found that a cruising speed of 55-60mph was comfortable.

By June 1946 Regency Red and Shires Green had joined Black as options for the paintwork. The interior of red cars was red and the green cars green but, as previously, buyers of black vehicles could chose any of the three options of interior colour. The price, however, had risen to £412.10.0, to which was then added the newly introduced purchase tax. By comparison, the last quoted price for the TB when the last few cars produced were sold in April 1940 was £247.10.0.

When *The Motor* in 1947 subjected a car to a full road test, they also commented on improvements and were impressed by the quality of the finish of the car. The leather interior and polished wooden dashboard with its full range of instruments, allied to the stability, comfort and performance - for an all-inclusive price of £527.16.8d - they thought the car excellent value and the cheapest true sports car on the market. Looked at today, a time of over 21secs

A batch of new TCs being collected by drivers from the Derbyshire Police.

Details from the more lavish booklet issued towards the end of TC production.

to reach 60mph seems very slow, but when compared to the average small saloon car of the period this was real performance. It was only when the crop of more aerodynamic sports cars arrived that the TC began to look really outclassed.

So what is this car like to drive now? Stepping out of an MGB or Midget, the first thing you notice is that getting into the car and working your way past the large steering requires a certain technique. The doors are hinged at the back, which demands an approach to the seat from a different direction. With that sorted out, even taller drivers will find enough room if the seat is set right back. This involves co-ordination between driver and passenger as both the seat bases must be adjusted together and the seat backrest pushed back on the adjusters fixed to both rear wheel-arches.

The brake and clutch pedals sprout from the floor but the accelerator pedal is pivoted to the firewall and has a neat roller on the end for the right foot. The layout of the pedals allows for easy simultaneous operation of the brake and throttle pedals but there is no room to rest the left foot except on the clutch pedal. The steering wheel is large and is often of the aftermarket Brooklands type. These were fitted at the time as accessories to many

The engine on the TC is easily accessible. All the early cars had the bulkhead painted light grey and the engine dark grey but this car is finished in the style of all the later cars - the bulkhead is body colour and the engine dark red. This car has one of the aluminium rocker covers sold by accessory dealers and a heat shield to try to reduce a tendency for heat from the exhaust manifold to affect the flow of modern fuels to the carburettors.

Earlier headlamp with pre-war style of glass.

TCs. The dashboard layout places the tachometer, with its inset electric clock, right in front of the driver, and the speedometer is over to the left-hand side of the car for the passenger to observe if the speed limits were being broken. No left-hand drive TCs were built by the factory. To warn the driver when he was exceeding the limit there was also a Lucas Thirtylite fitted to the dashboard that lit at about 20mph and went out at

1947 London Motor Show magazine advertisement, with the YA saloon that was also built at Abingdon.

A later model TC in Ivory with red trim. As was usual practice with the TC, the radiator slats are painted the same colour as the trim. The Midget mascot fitted to the radiator cap was a popular accessory for all MGs prior to the TF. The spot lamp is not correct.

An early TC with tan hood and twin rear windows.

30mph. This lamp had a matching map reading light on the passenger side, but overseas cars were fitted with two map lamps.

All the controls and smaller instruments are grouped on an attractive instrument panel in the centre of the dashboard. There is an ammeter and an oil pressure gauge but a water temperature gauge could later be added as an aftermarket extra. The ignition key fitted into a knob that also controls the sidelights and headlamps. Alongside this is a combined horn button and dipswitch. The horn push is within easy reach of the steering wheel rim and the horn itself is mounted on one of the badge bar brackets fitted to the front apron.

The starter knob operates a cable attached to a switch fixed directly on the starter motor, with the mixture knob alongside to enrich the twin SU carburettors. On the TC the mixture control does not raise the idle speed when pulled, this being achieved by twisting the knob to increase the speed. There are switches for the front fog-lamp and the instrument panel lights, together with the usual ignition warning light and a pair of plug sockets to provide power for an inspection lamp. These were popular accessories. There is no fuel gauge but a warning lamp on the right-hand side of the dashboard starts to flash when about three gallons are left in the13-gallon tank and remains permanently lit when it falls to below two gallons.

Earlier TC with wood veneered dashboard.

The last TC Midget leaves the Abingdon assembly line still in need of some components.

The engine is fairly firmly mounted in the chassis and some vibration is transmitted through the steering wheel and body but this only combines with the deep exhaust note to give the impression of a power unit larger than only 1250cc. The clutch is operated by a pedal connected to a lever attached to a cross shaft in the bell housing. This gives a smooth, snatch-free action. The engine revs freely and in spite of only producing 54bhp, aided by a superb gearbox, is quite capable of keeping up with modern traffic on winding A and B roads. The gearbox has well spaced ratios and synchromesh on all but first gear. Changes can be made fairly quickly, although those more used to modern cars will notice that if these are rushed too much the gear teeth will protest.

The rear axle ratio fitted to the TC gives just under 16mph per 1000 revs in top gear. A popular modification is to fit the TA rear axle ratio of 4.875:1 to give nearly 1mph extra at the same engine speed. As the engine spins so freely it is quite comfortable cruising at around 4000rpm although a careful watch on the oil pressure gauge is prudent on motorways. Five-speed gearbox conversions are gaining favour, but do mean that cars may be marked down if entered in concours at club meetings.

Unlike all later MGs, the TC does not have rack and pinion steering and the Bishop Cam steering box fitted can suffer from wear. A good TC will have a small amount of free movement at the steering wheel but will steer very accurately and, although heavy at parking speed, the steering lightens up at speed. The car will steer straight and will not be put off line by bumps provided the front axle is correctly fitted and straight, and provided the taper wedges fitted to later TCs to lighten the amount of strength need to turn the wheel are removed. More modern steering boxes have been fitted to some cars. Unfortunately most

Home market TC with later lights alongside a YA saloon.

Front of a new TC parked in the street.

Hood windows in a new TC parked in the street. A single D-lamp was standard, not now legal.

TCs will have passed through many hands and perhaps been rebuilt more than once. They may contain few of the parts fitted when built and thus will often not feel as good on the road as a truly original, low mileage example, something now almost never found.

The bench seat is very comfortable and insulates the driver and passenger quite well from bumpy roads. The ride is firm and the beam front axle is not as forgiving as the later independent front suspension, but the car holds the road well even on the narrow 19-inch wheels and tyres. After modern MGs you feel you are sitting much higher and the cut-away doors add to the feeling of sitting on the car, rather than in it, but on cold days the side-screens do give good protection and if the hood is raised this has a reasonable amount of headroom. So here we have a Midget that is good to look at and simple and easy to work on, with design and technology dating in part as far back as the early 1930s. It is, nevertheless, still quite capable of covering high mileages in comparative comfort,

A consignment of cars in November 1947 in front of The Saracens Head in Beaconsfield en route from Nuffield Exports in Oxford to London Docks for a boat to Los Angeles.

Early publicity picture probably taken in the countryside near the factory

once the driver accepts that it will feel a lot different from driving a modern car.

Once production began there were times when the supply of components became difficult and the factory even resorted to building three TC rolling chassis with van bodies to use to chase up parts. However, perhaps because of the 30mph speed limit then imposed on all on commercial vehicles, this was not a success and all three later had standard bodies fitted and were sold second hand via MG distributors.

As shown in the lists at the end of this section, there were some quite noticeable alterations to the TC during the time it was in production and the exact change points for many of these is uncertain. At the start of production the cars were much closer to the TB in detail than the final cars built. This is understandable because when post-war production increased at MG and at the component suppliers, changes to design and specification were inevitable. However, in these changes there are a number of pitfalls for the unwary restorer. For example, the shape of both the front and rear wings was modified quite substantially and it is quite possible to have a set of wings that don't match. The early front wings, for example, are closer to the TB design, but not identical, and the leading edge on these early wings is cut back further in front of the headlights than the later wings, giving a more pronounced peak above the front wheels.

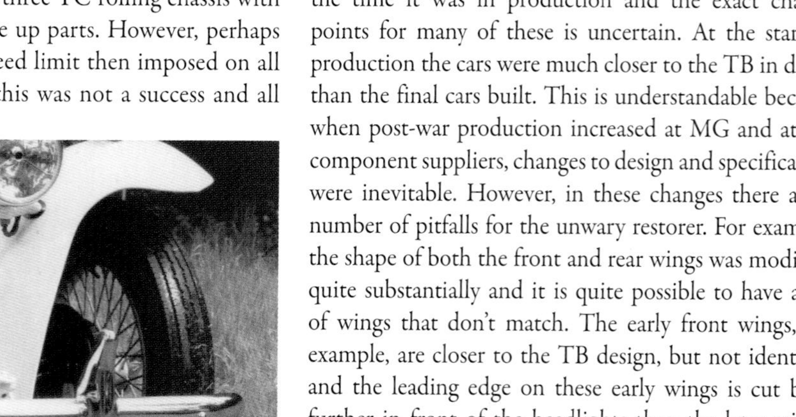

As already mentioned, all the early cars were black, but towards the end of 1946 red and green paint could be specified, and later Sequoia Cream and Clipper Blue were added to the range. Very noticeable was a change to the finish of the dashboard that occurred at chassis number TC5380 in April 1948. The attractive walnut

Front of one of the TCs built to meet American conditions. A solid bumper was fitted to protect the car from careless parkers. This model also had smaller 7-inch headlamps capable of taking sealed-beam light units.

veneered dashboard was superseded by one covered in Rexine to match the trim panels. Around this time the centre instrument panel and the bases of the lamps changed from black to metallic tan.

Other detail changes were made during the production run of the car. For example, the section of the rear wings also changed, with the later cars having wings of a slightly less rounded section that gave them a wider appearance. The headlamps on the TC are very prominent and the first 1600 cars were fitted with the TB style lamps with fairly flat glasses incorporating a U-pattern lens. Later cars had different rims and the glass was much more dished, giving a rounded appearance to the front of the lamp. The fog lamp similarly changed at chassis number TC4740 from the pre-war style Lucas FT27 to the bulkier SFT 462 fog lamp. These were also available as an extra on the TD.

Under the bonnet the engine was not modified at all, but the colour and design of the pressed steel scuttle was amended. Approximately half way through production the shape of the flutes on the scuttle changed to ones that were much shallower, and the colour was altered from a light grey on all cars to being painted to match the colour of the body. The engine colour was also changed about this time from dark grey to deep red. Early engines often were fitted with a smart aluminium rocker cover in place of the more usual pressed steel one, and many owners subsequently purchased and fitted similar covers from parts suppliers both at home and in the United States and other overseas markets.

Strong mounting brackets for the bumper were bolted to the front of the chassis side rails.

The special model for the United States carried the chassis plate designation EX-U (Export United States) and was only built towards the end of production of the TC at a time when exports had increased considerably. In 1946, for example, 674 cars of the total 1675 cars built were exported, but by 1948 this had risen to 2788 out of a total build of 3085. To meet local conditions the cars were fitted with full width bumpers with overriders. These bumpers were fixed to the ends of the chassis rails and were similar to, but not the same

The TC EX-U rear bumper with the cast MG badge fitted to the centre. This model also had twin rear lights fitted to brackets alongside the top of the fuel tank side plates.

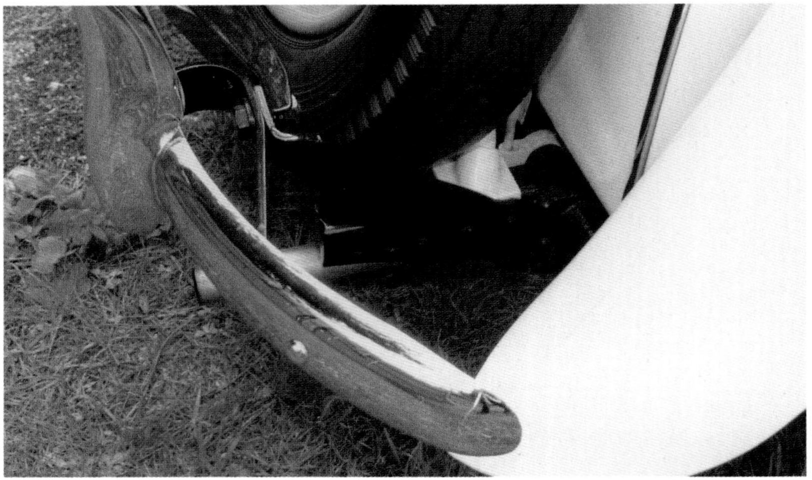

The rear bumper was mounted on strong brackets bolted to the chassis side rails

as, those later fitted to the TD. The centre of the back bumper had a plinth with a cast MG badge with raised lettering fixed to it.

To accommodate sealed beam headlamps, smaller 7-inch Lucas S700 type lamps, as used for the TD, were fitted and the front fog lamp was deleted – the position of its dashboard switch was taken by a high beam warning light. To improve the lighting at the rear of the car, the single combined brake and side light was replaced by a pair of high-mounted circular lamps fitted each side of the petrol tank on special brackets. These and the front sidelights also doubled as flashing indicators with those at the rear using a pair of brake switch override relays to interrupt the brake light circuit. The position normally occupied by the inspection lamp sockets on the instrument panel was used to mount the flasher switch.

As well as removing the fog lamp from the badge bar brackets, the horn was also moved. It was replaced by a pair of scuttle-mounted horns, one high and one low note, as fitted later on the TD. The positions of the other dials and switches were also changed. As these cars were all built during the final couple of years of production they had the fabric covered dashboards and metallic tan instrument panels without any lettering, and most were fitted with a three-spoke steering wheel finished in a similar colour. Any buyers of cars from America should be aware that some changes to what is accepted standard specification should be retained as the factory might have done them when the cars were built.

TC In Competition

For most of the time the TC was being built, promoting sales by entering them in competition events was not seen as a priority. The MG brand was being publicised to some extent by the record-breaking efforts of Gardner with EX135, but this was mainly a private enterprise with very limited factory

The early TC bought new by Dick Jacobs running in an event after he had fitted a supercharger and aluminium cycle wings and bonnet.

The result of the transformation of his TC was a pretty sports/racing car that betrayed little of its origins. George and Barbara Phillips drove the car to Le Mans.

support. The most prominent competitors using TC-based specials was George Phillips, who used his TC special to run at Le Mans and elsewhere. Dick Jacobs was another to successfully compete in his TC in events at Silverstone and elsewhere. These efforts came to the notice of Abingdon and the factory started to provide them with some limited assistance.

The BRDC and the *Daily Express* were keen to promote a genuine production car race and Dick and George tried to interest the MG Car Company in providing a team of standard cars. John Thornley was eventually persuaded to enter three TCs with Dick, George and Ted Lund as drivers. The 1949 race was held at Silverstone and the drivers were instructed to report to the factory on the Thursday before the race to collect the three cream bog-standard TCs, which they were drive in convoy to the circuit after a parade through Oxford with the three Rileys that were

As a result of the publicity earned by their efforts in TC-based specials, Dick Jacobs and George Phillips were offered a drive in the Production Car Race at Silverstone in 1949 with Ted Lund the third driver. The three-car TC team were placed second, third and fourth in the 1500cc class.

also entered by Abingdon.

After a fraught practice session where the cars cornered badly with their standard wheels and tyres, Dick persuaded John Thornley to deviate from specification to the extent of binding the rear springs to stiffen them and fitting 16-inch rear wheels. In the race the cars ran well, finishing in fifth, sixth and seventh places and averaging nearly 70mph. That was not bad as the top speed of a standard TC was only around 75mph. This modest success persuaded John to provide the drivers with MGs to use in production car events for the 1950 season.

In America the TC is said to have sparked interest in MG sports cars and in similar cars from other manufacturers. However, one has to remember that in the late 1930s MGs imported and raced by the likes of Miles Collier had already sown the seeds of sports car racing on street circuits and elsewhere. In 1948 the entries for the first of the races held on the streets of Watkins Glen included eleven MGs and after qualifying in a preliminary race over four laps of the 6.6-mile circuit six TCs finished in the first ten. The highest-placed three TCs were all supercharged, with the Briggs Cunningham car ahead of those driven by Sam and Miles Collier. In the main race the three supercharged TCs finished in third, fourth and fifth places with the unsupercharged cars in sixth, eighth and tenth places. The event was continued in subsequent years with MGs filling part of the grid.

In 1948 the entries for the first of the races held on the streets of Watkins Glen included eleven MGs.

Changes In Production

Mechanical

Approx. XPAG/2020 to approx. XPAG/2965: within this range of engines some were given an attractive cast and polished aluminium rocker cover with octagonal oil filler cap in place of the pressed steel original. Many other engines were later given similar covers sold by accessory firms.

TC 2196	Speedometer cable re-routed.
TC 3856	Hydraulic dampers added to carburettors
TC 4251	Tapered packing added between axle pads and springs to reduce steering effort.
TC 5039	Steering drop arm modified.

Electrical

TC1850 (approx.)	Headlamps with more rounded glasses. Rims also changed.
TC 3414	Control box changed from Lucas RF91to RF95/2, which required another hole be drilled in the bulkhead
TC 4739	Fog lamp changed from FT27 to SFT 462

Other Changes

TC 5000 (approx.)	Bulkhead now had shallower flutes and was body colour not grey. Doorsill plates no longer carried 'MG Car Company' lettering.
TC 5178 (approx.)	Half tonneau cover changed from black to fawn.
TC 5380	Fabric to match trim replaced walnut veneer on dashboard. The centre panel and lamp bases colour changed from gold to black

Specification TC

Wheelbase/track	7' 10"/3' 9"
Suspension	Leaf springs front and rear
Wheels/tyres	Centre-laced Rudge type 2.50" x 19"/4.50"x19"
Brake drum size	9 inch
Engine/power output	1250cc/54bhp
Gearbox	4-speed synchromesh on top three ratios
Build dates	17th September 1945 to 29th November 1949
Cars built	10,000

The TD Midget

The MG Car Company established its reputation as England's premier builder of small sports cars during the heady days of competition and record braking successes of the 1930s. However, it produced comparatively small numbers of each model and it was only when the post-war T-types arrived that each model of Midget was produced in really large numbers. The TC had been rushed into production in 1945 with only minor modifications to the pre-war TB design. In spite of being out of date from the outset, such was the post-war thirst for cars, and particularly sports cars, that by 1949 10,000 examples had sold. This was three times the number of TAs and TBs built pre-war, and up to then no MG had sold in such large numbers.

However, the real achievement of the TC was to introduce a new generation to British sports cars. The time was right. Post-war reconstruction, and continuing high spending by governments on advanced armaments in the nuclear arms race with the Soviet Union, provided full employment and high wages, particularly in overseas markets like the United States. However, despite being right-hand drive, buyers must have enjoyed the change from the usual American cars because sales of the TC increased in that country to such an extent that by 1948 the company felt the need to build a special US version which was equipped with bumpers and flashing turn indicators to suit local conditions. These still were not left-hand drive, but this was to come with the TC's replacement, the TD.

The TC chassis design was seen as outdated once the Y-type saloon was announced in early 1947. This new saloon was built alongside the TC at Abingdon but, whilst retaining the traditional MG radiator, separate headlamps and flowing wings, it had a thoroughly modern chassis. As a means of obtaining good roadholding, most pre-war sports cars had the springs as stiff as possible and the chassis frames kept fairly flexible to accommodate the twisting necessary to help keep all four wheels on the ground. Unfortunately this caused stress to the bodywork with consequent cracks in metal cladding and paintwork damage.

That said, the roadholding of those pre-war cars was good, especially on smooth roads, but by the late 1930s designers had realised that a more rigid chassis allied to softer springs and independent suspension was a better option, especially for the front wheels.

An early TD without ventilation holes in the disc wheels.

The attractive brochure for the later TD with pierced wheesl.

One of the first TDs was used for a fashion shoot in London. The lack of traffic at the time going down The Mall made this view possible

In 1935, with the R-type, MG had experimented with an all-independent car, and had also designed a similarly sprung road car, but the sale of the company later that year by Lord Nuffield to the parent Nuffield Group killed that project, and future MGs were consigned to use more standard components from within the Morris empire. In 1938 what was post-war to be the YA chassis was used for an MG version of the Morris Eight saloon powered by the XPAG engine. That car was put on the back burner once it became obvious that war was imminent and it formed the basis of the 1940s YA. The engine went to power the stopgap model TB Midget in twin SU carburettor, 1250cc guise.

The first TD leaflet showed a car with unventilated wheels and was marked 'provisional.

The Y-type chassis was made up of welded, closed box-section side rails and tubular cross members. At the back it ran under the rear axle, which was suspended on leaf springs and had a Panhard rod to give lateral location. At the front a cross member housed the coil springs and provided a mounting for the rack and pinion steering gear. The basic design of the front suspension, utilising coil springs, lower wishbones and with the shock absorbers providing the upper mounting for the swivel pins, was to continue right through to the end of production of the MGB. The body used Morris Eight panels, fitted to a separate chassis, but the longer bonnet and the Abingdon radiator gave it an improved appearance. The pressed steel wheels, rather than the wires fitted to previous MGs, were a radical departure but the average owner must have blessed the ease with which they could be cleaned.

The YA was powered by a single carburettor version of the XPAG engine fitted to the TC. As the car weighed over a ton when laden, and the engine produced just 46 bhp, performance was adequate rather than sprightly. However, the Y-type was very well received by the motoring press who were at pains to point out the advantages of the independent front suspension and the stiffer chassis.

Having the Y-type built alongside the TC made it obvious that a redesign of the Midget sports model

A batch of new TDs en-route to the docks to be shipped overseas.

was long overdue. The strength of overseas MG sales, especially in North America, made it imperative that any new car should be able to be built in both right- and left=hand drive form without too many production line difficulties. In the event it was the Y-type chassis that provided the inspiration for the new TD. Initial experiments with a shortened saloon chassis fitted with a TC body were carried out at the factory before the drawings for the new car were done in the design office at Cowley. The TD chassis was similar to the Y-type at the front end but it swept over the leaf-sprung rear axle with the YA Panhard

Restored early TD painted in the popular combination of red with tan leather seat covers.

A magazine advertisement placed in issues on sale at the time of the London Motor Show.

rod omitted. In common with most other Nuffield products, the rear axle itself was a hypoid unit, also later fitted to the YB saloon. The braking system was an improvement over the TC, with twin leading shoes on the front brakes and a fly-off hand brake mounted on the central tunnel and operating the rear brake shoes via twin cables.

The TD body was made roomier than the TC and its construction incorporated a pressed steel rear bulkhead behind the seats that provided a far more rigid mounting for the rear door pillars. The rear wings were bolted to the inner wings in the body structure using built in captive nuts, an improvement over the wood screws used for that purpose on the TC. Because the TD used smaller wheels, the wings themselves were deeper, giving the car a more solid appearance. A wider fuel tank, a more steeply sloping spare wheel mounting and the rear valance covering the chassis rails added to this impression.

For the first time on an MG sports car, bumpers and overriders appeared as standard equipment. The bumpers were carried on bumper bars bolted directly to the rear chassis rails and to extensions of the front chassis frame. These additions gave the TD the strength

Posed publicity picture taken in Long Crendon village location near to the Abingdon factory.

With the models dressed in the current fashion, the TD was photographed in an attractive location

to protect the front and back of the TD Midget from the odd parking knocks and were particularly welcome in America where many of the TCs previously sold had to have bumpers added later to protect the cars bodywork.

From the outset the TD could be built with the steering wheel on the left-hand side for some overseas markets. Unlike the later MGA, the chassis for the right- and left-hand drive cars differed as the pedal box and pivot shaft mounting bush were welded to it. However, as many who have subsequently converted the cars will testify, it is a comparatively easy task to make the change. The rack and pinion steering was carried over from the Y-type, although the pinion shaft is longer than that used on the saloon. This steering gear is ideally suited to the TD and gives precise steering and secure handling, which is enhanced by the availability of radial ply tyres, albeit

A restored later TD with a three-bow hood frame that provided increased headroom over the previous two-bow type

Posed by an impressive set of gates, a later TD is photographed for publicity purposes

often only from specialist suppliers.

Steel disc wheels were perhaps the one feature of the TD that was not universally popular. Particularly overseas, the perception was that sports cars should have wire wheels, and these were never an optional extra on the TD. When the TF was introduced, wire wheels were offered as an option and many cars where fitted with them. At the same time kits were sold to convert TDs to wire wheels, but these do not improve the appearance of the car. Somehow, although they look right on TFs, they do not suit the lines of the TD, which always looks better on the standard disc wheels. After about 500 cars were built, the appearance of the disc wheels was improved when they had cooling holes punched in them. It is quite rare now to see one of the earlier cars with plain disc wheels.

The interior of the car was very similar to the TC but the wider cockpit gave the occupants a little more comfort. As with the earlier cars, the interior trim was available in either red, green or tan leather seat facings with the dashboard trimmed to match. A useful addition was the small glove box, although if the optional valve radio was specified this filled the space inside it. The area behind the seats was just large enough to stow a small suitcase or a few soft bags, but for serious touring a luggage rack could be ordered. The four sidescreens stowed in a compartment at the back of the luggage area but care was needed when fitting them in the box as it was all too easy to scratch the Perspex windows. The hood gave adequate weather protection when fitted and the headroom was later improved with the adoption of a three-bow hood frame in place of the two-bow one first used.

The speedometer and tachometer were placed in front of the driver with the oil pressure gauge and ammeter on the centre panel. Later the oil pressure gauge was combined with a water temperature gauge. As with the TC, the horn push was on this panel and on early cars it also incorporated a headlamp dipswitch. Later this was moved to a foot-operated switch. One change TC owners would notice on the TD was the adoption of a combined mixture enrichment and fast idle control. On the TC these were separate, but for the TD a more familiar choke control provided both a richer mixture and increased the idle speed. The panel had a switch for the front fog lamp, although on TDs this was always only an optional extra.

That rear spare wheel mounting mentioned earlier is a particularly substantial device; fixed at the lower end to the rear chassis and at the top to the rear of the bodywork it also has a mounting for the rear number plate incorporated. This mounting can be switched over for left-hand drive cars. In rear end collisions the tubular framework and the rigidly fixed spare wheel provide good protection for the fuel tank and the occupants of the car.

The penalty for all this strength and extra comfort for the passengers was an increase in weight of about 160lbs for the new car over the TC. As the engine was virtually unchanged, apart from the introduction of the then fashionable oil bath air cleaner, performance was only maintained by a reduction of the rear axle ratio. This change reduced the miles per hour per 1000rpm to 14.4 against the TC that did 15.5. This low gearing is, perhaps, the only feature of the TD that can cause problems on modern roads and many owners

Needed to prove the model was generally on sale to permit the tuned model to enter production car events, only 250 copies were printed of the brochure for the TD Mark II.

have fitted higher-ratio back axle gears or five-speed gearbox conversions to make motorway driving more pleasant.

The road testers of the time had no such qualms and gave the new car high praise. *The Autocar* writers said, 'The Series TD may be new, but it still looks like an MG and has not gone futuristic, for which many thanks, people will say. A sports car ought to look like a sports car and its innards ought to be accessible so that fans can personally keep it in tune; they should not be hidden beneath billows of bent tin.' Mind you, the same magazine was ecstatic about the MGA with its all-enveloping bodywork just five years later!

The test team recorded a time of 23.5 seconds to reach 60mph, which was a little slower than the rival *The Motor* magazine had recorded for the previous model, but when that magazine got their hands on the same TD a few weeks later they recorded a time of 21.3 seconds, so either the car had freed up a bit by then or *The Motor* testers had heavier right feet. The ride comfort and handling received favourable comments. *The Autocar* said, 'There is a marked feeling of increased solidity about the car, resulting from the new, and more rigid, frame, yet it has gained enormously in comfort of riding over the types of surfaces such as a car of this kind is likely to be asked to tackle.'

Other publications were equally enthusiastic and *Good Motoring*, for example, said that 'the most noticeable feature about the TD is the much improved ride given by the front suspension. Former Midget models were built for the enthusiast rather than for those who insisted on maximum comfort. In the TD the road inequalities are ironed out to the extent that any former critic of MG suspension would now applaud the good riding quality of the car at speed over any type of road surface.'

The April 1950 sales brochure gives the basic UK price as £455 plus £124.7.3 purchase tax, but initially most of the cars produced were exported. Records show that in 1949 just two of the 98 cars built stayed here, and in 1950 the situation was a little better with 149 of the 4767 built reaching the home market. It is not surprising, therefore, that until the recent re-importation of a large number of cars TDs had been comparatively rare in this country.

Buyers lucky enough to lay their hands on one of the new cars had initially the choice of paintwork in Black, MG Red, Ivory, Clipper Blue and Almond Green. In 1951 the range of colours was increased to include Autumn Red – a darker shade than MG Red – and Sun Bronze metallic, which was also available on the Y-type but used on only a very few TDs. In 1952 the range of colours was changed again and was now Black, MG Red, Ivory and Woodland Green – a darker colour than Almond Green. In addition there were a few cars painted in Silver Streak Grey metallic. The three upholstery colours, green, red and tan, were all available with Black paintwork; red and tan with red paintwork, green and tan on the green cars and red or green on the ivory cars. Sun Bronze and Silver cars had red upholstery. In all cases the hoods were made from tan Wigan cloth.

The popularity of the TD, especially in the United States, led to its becoming the best selling MG so

Cut-away drawing in a TD brochure.

The twin SU fuel pumps fitted to the TD Mark II.

The attractive TD dashboard that was covered in Rexine to match the cockpit trim, dished dials for speedometer and tachometer, three-spoke steering wheel and neat glove box.

The Andrex friction additional shock absorbers fitted as standard to the TD Mark II.

far. It outsold the TC, with around 30,000 cars built and sold, of which only 1656 stayed in the United Kingdom. The United States imported 23,488 and quite a number of these still survive.

As the most numerous of the T-types, the TD has, nevertheless, been overshadowed here by the later TF, which many consider a more attractive car. However, the TD is in many ways a nicer car to drive. The better dashboard layout and more adjustable seating make the driver feel very comfortable. The bonnet gives better access to the engine and also has more air space around it to help cooling. Finally, and perhaps most importantly,

A restored TD Mark II finished in its original colour scheme of green with green trim.

The TD Mark II had larger size twin SU carburettors and a different air cleaner than the ordinary TD.

TDs often now do not cost as much as TFs.

So that is the TD. Not the fastest car in its day, nor perhaps the prettiest, but certainly a thoroughly honest sports car that performed well and was strong enough to stand up to almost anything drivers all over the world did to it. TDs are still popular cars but only their owners perhaps appreciate just how practical and comfortable they can be. These Midgets combine some of the charm of pre-war looks with the practicality of a more modern chassis, fairly good brakes and a strong engine that is also capable of being modified to increase power output.

Towards the end of TD production the Mark II TDs carried this badge on the rear bumper and on both sides of the bonnet. Also the MG badges on the radiator nosepiece and spare wheel were black and white, rather than cream and brown.

TDs going to America being unloaded from a railway wagon by a warehouse at Liverpool Docks.

This Export LHD TD chassis went down the line at Abingdon 25th July 1951 and was sent to Germany where a locally made copy of the usual factory coachwork was fitted.

The interior trim of the Stuttgart TDs differs from that fitted at Abingdon.

The TD Special Bodied Cars

From the earliest days of motoring and right up until after the Second World War it was quite common for the manufacture of the complete and running rolling chassis to be entirely separate from making, painting and trimming the bodywork. Coachbuilders, often firms that had been in existence since the days of horse-drawn carriages, vied with each other to build car bodywork, either directly for the car manufacturer or for the dealer selling the car, who was usually working for a particular client.

After the war the remaining coachbuilders survived, in the main by diversifying, often by offering modifications to standard products. There were still some coachbuilt Rolls-Royces with bodies made by firms like James Young and Barker, but numbers were small. Harold Radford, a West London Rolls-Royce and Bentley dealer, bucked the trend by actually getting into the trade after the war with his upmarket estate car versions of the Mark VI Bentley. These initially had wood-framed bodies built by an outside firm, but later were modified standard saloons. Other firms prospered, like Abbotts of Farnham, who first built bodies for Healey chassis and later moved over to making estate car versions of Ford cars, and Jensen, who made sports versions of the A40 for Austin and later bodies fitted to the big Austin-Healey sports cars; from 1957 these were shipped to Abingdon for finishing.

Sales of MGs as chassis did resume for a time after the war, although as a reduced volume of total sales.

The Ferrari Barchetta style body fitted by Weidenhausen to a RHD TD chassis.

Records show that ten TCs were sold like this, but to what end is not recorded. However, more TDs did leave as rolling chassis and these, together with eleven YAs and YBs and two TFs, were the last MGs to leave Abingdon in this form. There were nine right-hand drive and 157 left-hand drive TD rolling chassis sent from Abingdon, and in addition many complete cars were later re-bodied by their owners, usually to better suit them to competition work. It is outside the scope of this book to examine the latter, but we will look here at some of those that received non-standard bodies from new.

One of the reasons for exporting MGs in chassis form, both before and after the war, was to reduce some of the import duties imposed by governments keen to support local companies building car, van and truck bodies. An interesting example of this is the Cologne car importers, J.A. Woodhouse, who brought in around 40 TDs as chassis and commissioned Hennefarth of Bad Cannstatt to make what to outward appearances were ordinary standard TDs. However, probably because they were working without factory body drawings, they differed in detail from the Abingdon product. Much of the metalwork in the body was made locally and items like the electrical equipment were of German manufacture. Also some parts were polished aluminium, not chromed brass or steel. The same coachbuilder also fitted a more modern looking body to a new TD chassis for a customer.

Another German coachbuilder was Wendler of Reutlingen, also known for their work on the Porsche 550 and on special estate car bodies for VW beetles, who built three special TDs for an MG dealer in Heidelberg. One had a shape reminiscent of the Jaguar XK120 and the other two were more slab-sided. All carried MG style radiator grilles. There was a fourth TD from the same coachbuilder built to a private commission and this was a very distinctive closed coupé with its headlamps set within a very non-MG grille. In Germany there were three other TD chassis completed locally, two by Schloemer of Cologne, a coupé and a cabriolet, and one roadster in the style of the Ferrari Barchetta by Weidenhausen in Frankfurt.

In Italy before the conflict there had been a fairly flourishing coachbuilding industry and this continued when peace returned. There was, however, a shortage of work available from local car manufacturers and having MG Y-type and TD chassis available must have been seen as an opportunity. Rocco Motto of Turin was a coachbuilder, in business since the early 1930s. Working usually behind the scenes for larger manufacturers, Motto became associated with elegant designs. In the 1940s it constructed some bodies for Fiat, Cisitalia and Alfa-Romeo chassis and became well known, even in America. This led to an order through a New York MG dealer for a body for a TD similar to that he had made for Cisitalia.

The Turin Motor Show, an event only revived after industry lobbying, provided a shop window for Italian

A postcard was printed for the Arnolt TD to promote sales.

Brochure for Arnolt TD.

The very clean lines of the Arnolt are enhanced in this example by the Borrani wire wheels, an optional extra.

The Arnolt TD Coupé is an attractive car with only the wheels to hint at TD underpinnings.

designers and coachbuilders, and for 1952 Bertone, in collaboration with Franco Scaglione, decided to build cars on two TD chassis and designed very elegant coupé and convertible models. These cars were prepared and displayed on the stand of local Nuffield distributors, Fattori and Mantani of Rome. On the morning of the opening day Bertone was approached by an American, Stanley Arnolt, who said he would like to order a number of the cars for sale through his dealership in the United States. Having bought and sold a TC in 1949, Arnolt had in 1950 gone into the distribution of British cars for the American Mid-West from premises at 153 East Street, Chicago. His first consignment had consisted of 25 MGs, 20 Morris Minors and 6 RM Rileys.

He took the two TDs from the show back to the United States and displayed them to the American public at the Elkhart Lake Road Races in September 1952. One of the main selling points he made of the convertible was the ease with which the hood could be raised and the snug fit of the windows. He stressed that due to a combination of steel and aluminium in the body construction the cars weighed very little more than the standard TD and rather conservatively claimed that this was a mere 40lbs extra for the coupé and 20lbs for the roadster.

Arnolt also sold car accessories and held the concession for other makes of British cars, including Aston-Martin, Rolls Royce, Bentley and Bristol, and one of his other ventures was to have his own bodies made for the latter, creating the Arnolt-Bristol. This was produced in three versions, a basic open car with cut-down windscreen, an up-market version with full windscreen, hood, etc., and a coupé model.

For quite a bit more cash, those who bought the Arnolt Coupé travelled in much greater comfort than they would in a standard TD. The usual instruments were supplied with the rolling chassis, but the panel was fitted the other way up in the Arnolt, flanked by the speedometer and tachometer.

A brochure produced for the Ghia-Aigle. It must have been thought that more than just three cars would be built.

It appears that rolling chassis for the Arnolt-MGs were delivered from Abingdon in batches, all carrying the MG guarantee plate bolted to the toe-board support box. With the chassis came the usual TD dashboard instruments and switches. The finished cars carried an Arnolt number and Bertone body number as well as the MG chassis number. As the bodies were hand made, and varied to quite a degree, each item of trim was also marked with the Bertone number to ensure that it was fitted to the correct body. To add to the individuality, the standard TD dash panel was mounted upside down and flanked by the usual speedometer and tachometer. Borrani wire wheels, a radio and heater were on the options list.

Unlike the bolted-on standard wood-framed TD body tub, the main steel body frames of the Arnolt cars were welded to the chassis. The large doors hinged directly onto the steel body structure. Most of the panels were of hand-formed steel, but the doors, bonnet and boot had aluminium skins. Under the bonnet the engine installation was unchanged, as was the radiator mounting. The standard bracing bars for the radiator and toe-boards remained, but the engine compartment was lined with side panels ventilated by louvres, and an entirely different scuttle was installed.

The body shape produced less drag than the standard car, which helped to offset the weight increase. The well-trimmed interior was one of the most appealing features of an Arnolt. The higher door line and glass windows in the doors on the convertible gave the occupants less wind buffeting at speed. At the rear, the boot lid was released by a control behind the front passenger seat and opened to reveal a good-sized compartment, certainly roomy enough for weekend luggage. The rear-hinged bonnet was released by a pull mounted under the dashboard. Externally, the flush-fitting door handles were a neat touch. Many of the cars were fitted with the optional Italian Borrani wire wheels, with either steel or alloy rims, but towards the end of production some cars had Dunlop wire wheels.

The Arnolt appealed to a different type of purchaser from those buying the factory TD. The greater comfort, together with the ease of raising and lowering the soft top, brought the potential market for the car closer to that held by the Jaguar XK140 drophead and the American convertibles. Unfortunately the small 1250cc engine did not really give sufficient power to compete with these cars and fewer were built than originally envisaged, despite S.H. Arnolt Inc. having some 30 dealers in the US

One of the two open Ghia TDs photographed when new.

Rear view of the Ghia-Aigle Coupé designed, as were the open cars, by Giovanni Michelotti.

The Ghia-Aigle Coupé had the headlights mounted each side of the grille and additional ones in the top of the wings.

Brochure for the TDs converted by Inskip into four-seaters.

One of the TDs converted by Inskip of New York into a four-seater by adding ten inches to the length of the chassis. (Knudson picture)

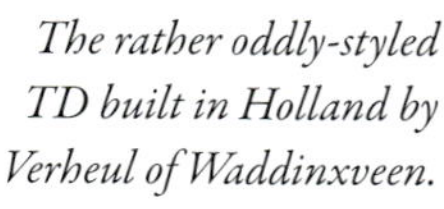

The rather oddly-styled TD built in Holland by Verheul of Waddinxveen.

Mid-West. The final production numbers have been variously quoted as 65 coupés and 35 convertibles or 67 coupés and 33 convertibles, not including the two prototypes, and the Arnolt TDs are, therefore by far the most numerous of the coachbuilt cars using that chassis.

Switzerland had been a good market for MG prior to 1939 with both complete cars and rolling chassis exported there, mainly through J.H. Keller AG of Zurich. When the Y-type chassis became available a number were imported and fitted with local bodywork, mainly to provide open versions prior to the introduction of the Abingdon-built four-seater Y-tourer. There appeared also to be a market for a more stylish version of the TD sports model and Ghia-Aigle of Switzerland built bodies for three TD chassis for sale through Keller.

At that time Giovanni Michelotti was the contracted designer and probably was instrumental in devising the attractive appearance of the two open cars and the single coupé the company built, all right-hand drive. The first open car was exhibited on the Nuffield/Keller stand at the 1953 Geneva Motor Show. The coupé was, perhaps, less attractive than the open cars and there was no provision to carry more than two people. The main headlights were fitted within the radiator grille, like the Wendler coupé, but there were also two more lights set in the tops of the front wings. On the other hand, the car obviously provided more comfortable accommodation than the standard MG, but at a price. Neither model created enough interest for the exercise to be repeated. Michelotti also designed an oddly styled coupé for a Swiss client in Lugano that bore a resemblance to the Ghia-Aigle cars, but with a heavier looking grille.

Alfredo Vignale, who previously had worked for Farina, in 1948 established a coachbuilding company in Turin. Better known for his Ferrari and Maserati creations, he was given the job of making the body for a right-hand drive MG chassis. Again this was just a one-off effort.

Of the other TD chassis exported to Europe some went to Holland, where a variety of quite different cars were produced, including for competition work. Veth and Zoon, a very long established coachbuilder in Arnhem still in existence today, built a body for a TD chassis that followed a style set by cars like the contemporary razor-edge Triumph Renown. In Austria the local Nuffield importer G.H. Perl fitted differing bodies to a number of left-hand drive TD chassis.

Probably not qualifying within the remit of this book, but nevertheless interesting as a variation from standard, are the four-seater TDs produced by

J.S. Inskip for sale through that distributor's dealers in New York. By then the four-seater open Y-types were no longer available and there was thought to be a market for a replacement. What the company did was to cut the standard car chassis at the door openings and lengthen it by around 10 inches. New longer doors were made and the front bench seat was removed and replaced with a pair of bucket seats with hinged backrests. A rear seat was fitted, along with a soft top that had a large rear window and was accompanied by suitable sidescreens. Chrome side strips on the body served to enhance the appearance of the car. The cost was $2925 at a time when the standard TD cost less than $2000 and it is said that the company made only around 12 examples.

Finally, one special TD is UMG 400, the car built at Abingdon for George Phillips to race in the 1951 Le Mans. After all the effort expended on its construction it is a pity that the engine failed early in the race. However, one outcome of the venture was that it may have inspired designer Syd Enever to do something about producing a chassis that allowed occupants to sit within the side frames, rather than perched above them, and this new chassis, plus some elements of the styling of UMG 400, went into EX175, the prototype for the MGA.

The TD In Competition

In spite of all the controls and restrictions placed on the company by virtue of being part of the Nuffield Group, there was still a desire to use the cars in competition and for any successes to be used by the MG Car Company as publicity. Even one of the first catalogues for the TD, dated December 1949, lists amongst the optional extras a twin spare wheel carrier and large-section rear tyres for trials, as well as double shock absorbers, twin SU fuel pumps and special tuning for the engine for road use and club competition events. To assist high speed running with tuned cars a 4.55:1 axle ratio could be specified as an alternative for the 5.125 gears that were standard.

Early in 1950 Dick Jacobs and George Phillips tried out a slightly modified TD for John Thornley, but found it too slow and with over-soft suspension for racing. Following discussions a more highly tuned version fitted with bucket seats and additional shock absorbers was produced and this car, FMO 885, was entered in the Blandford Production Car Race. After a ding-dong battle with Eric Thompson in an HRG, Dick finally won the race, but could not keep the trophy as MG were unable to confirm that at least six other cars to the same specification had been produced for sale. Most of the changes, plus others, were incorporated in the TD Mark II, a special version sold alongside the standard TD, thus allowing this model to be entered in future as a catalogued production car.

For the 1950 *Daily Express* Production Car Race at Silverstone three cars were entered. FRX 942 for George Phillips, FRX 943 for Ted Lund and FRX 941 for Dick Jacobs to drive. Despite a lot of work between

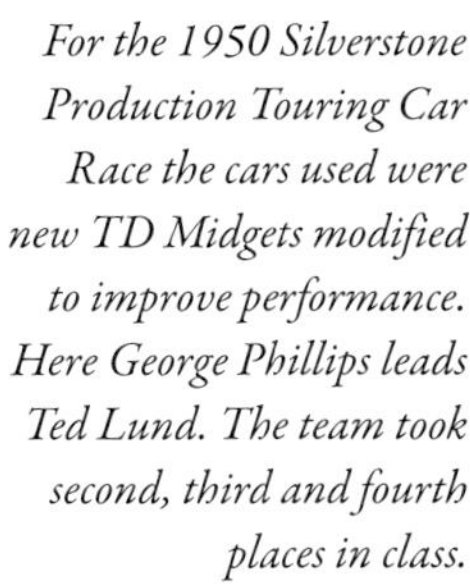

For the 1950 Silverstone Production Touring Car Race the cars used were new TD Midgets modified to improve performance. Here George Phillips leads Ted Lund. The team took second, third and fourth places in class.

In the Silverstone Daily Express *Production Car Race 1950, the TD number 18 was driven by Ted Lund.*

The TD special built at the factory for George Phillips to drive in the 1951 Le Mans Race.

practice and the race, lap times were only on a par with those achieved by the near-standard TCs the previous year. However, the final result for the 1500cc class was a win for Ruddocks' HRG with the MGs of Jacobs, Lund and Phillips in second third and fourth places. The same three modified TDs were then entered for the 1950 Tourist Trophy race run on the road circuit in Northern Island and were placed first, second and third in their class.

A TD engine was highly modified and fitted to the Goldie Gardner record car, EX135. This was taken to Utah in 1951, where it broke six International and ten USA National Records, along with two International and five American National Records, including in 1952 a new record for the 1km flying start of 202.14mph. Much was made of these successes in advertisements, especially in the United States, and this could have helped sales. In the early 1950s road racing, organised by the Sports Car Club of America, was very popular and both the TC and the TD dominated the entry lists in their class. Many cars were tuned and modified, and some very successful TD-based specials were built.

Dick Jacobs in the 1950 Tourist Trophy race run on the road circuit in Northern Island. The team of TDs were placed first, second and third in their class.

Ted Lund in the pits during the 1950 Tourist Trophy race.

The record-breaking feats by Goldie Gardner in EX135 provided both copy for newspaper reports and an opportunity to boost sales by MG dealers. Here the car is being delivered to the main Morris Garages showroom in Oxford

TD Changes In Production

Mechanical

XPAG/TD/2985	Purolator canister oil filter replaced with Wilmot Breedon oil filter
TD 4251	One-piece drum and hub introduced
TD 6035	Grease retaining seal changed from felt washer to steel cap
XPAG/TD/6482	Water pump modified
XPAG/TD/7576	Oil pick up moved to centre of sump
XPAG/TD/9008	Exhaust valve rocker arms modified
XPAG/TD2/9408	Change of clutch size and new bell housing prompts prefix change to TD2
XPAG/TD2/10900	Shorter dipstick and tube fitted
TD 11111	Steering rack inner tie rod housing modified
TD 12285	Threads on wheel studs, propshaft and back axle changed to unified. Studs and nuts on the spare wheel carrier were changed from car 12419
XPAG/TD2/14224	Much improved oil pump with integral replaceable oil filter introduced
XPAG/TD2/14948	New cast aluminium-finned sump with capacity increased from 9pints to 10.5pints introduced
XPAG/TD2/15861	Improved clutch lining introduced
XPAG/TD2/16482	Gearbox selector rails modified
XPAG/TD2/17289	Shorter pushrods with longer adjusting screws in rocker arms introduced
XPAG/TD2/17969	New cylinder block with round

water passage holes. New cylinder head gasket could also be used for earlier cars

XPAG/TD2/20942 Distributor fixing modified

XPAG/TD2/20972 Oil pump now has priming plug

XPAG/TD2/22717

TD 22251 clutch cable changed to stronger rod system

XPAG/TD2/22735 Cylinder head with round water passage holes. New head gasket and long reach spark plugs

XPAG/TD2/24116 New camshaft and revised valve timing. Tappet clearance changed from .19in to .12in and plate on side of rocker cover changed to reflect this

XPAG/TD2/244589 Oil pickup filter changed

XPAG/TD2/26635 New oil pump body

XPAG/TD2/27551 Improved crankshaft steel specification

XPAG/TD2/27867 Head machining changed to reduce height of valve spring seats to leave valve stems protruding more

XPAG/TD2/28167 Holes drilled to wire lock heads of bolts holding rocker shaft pedestals

Electrical

TD 7624 Headlamps on home market cars changed to left-hand dipping

TD 8142 TC type Lucas control box RF95/2 replaced with Lucas RB106/1 and separate SF6 fuse box

TD 21303 Rear lamps changed to circular type and rear wings changed to suit

TD 22315 Flashing indicators fitted to US market cars. Wiper motor moved to centre of windscreen top rail

Other changes

TD 0351 After only 100 cars produced a hoop fixed to the chassis was added to brace the scuttle

TD 0501 Solid steel wheels, as fitted to YB, replaced with ventilated type

TD 4237 Listed as the point when rubber mat fitted to left-hand drive cars. May also be the point when LHD pedals gained extension pieces and there was a recess cut in the floorboard to accommodate larger feet

TD 10751 LHD & TD 10779 RHD Speedometer and tachometer changed from flat faced chronomatic instruments to magnetic with dished dials. The ammeter also changed and a rheostat fitted for dimming the panel lights.

TD 13914 Combined oil pressure/water temperature gauge fitted

TD 17548 Headlamp high beam warning lamp fitted

TD 18883 Foot operated dipswitch fitted and horn button replaced combined horn/dip switch

TD 20374 LHD & TD 20696 RHD Three bow hood fitted and side-screen frames modified to suit

TD 20749 Additional mounting point fitted each side of the chassis, alongside the scuttle hoop, for fixing the body

Specification TD

Wheelbase/ track	7' 10"/Front 3' 11⅜" Rear 4' 2"
Suspension	Front Independent with coil springs and wishbones
	Rear Leaf springs
Wheels/tyres	Pressed steel with cooling holes from TD 0501
Brake drum size	9 inch
Engine/ power output	1250cc/54bhp
Gearbox	4-speed synchromesh on top three ratios
Build dates	10th November 1949 to 17th August 1953
Cars built	Standard cars 28,643
	Mark II 1022
	Rolling chassis and CKD kits 250

The TF Midget

The TF Midget is not the most numerous model of MG. However, if there were prizes available for the MG design that has been most admired and copied, then the TF made from 1953 until 1955 would very likely take first place. A unique blend of pre-war tradition and the more streamlined look that became fashionable in the late 1940s produced a timeless design that has ever since been admired and copied all over the world. With its immediate predecessor, the TD model launched in 1949, it has inspired the production of more replicas than any other car, aside from the legendary AC Cobra. Even now there is probably a kit car manufacturer somewhere in the world churning out parts for their particular TF pastiche. In Britain, the Naylor TF was probably the best known.

The prototype TF photographed in the design department at Cowley. The louvres on the bonnet tops were perhaps seen as a solution to reduce the temperature in the confined space around the engine.

Despite its undoubted appeal to later generations of sports car enthusiasts, at the time the TF was produced it was seen by many as outdated and to be merely a face-lifted TD that had been introduced to try to maintain sales whilst the British Motor Corporation came to grips with the fact that what was really needed was a completely new car. This impression was reinforced by the announcement of the revised Midget at the London Motor Show in October 1953, coinciding with launch of another brand new MG model. Visitors could not fail to compare the sleek, modern design and monocoque body/chassis of the Gerald Palmer designed ZA Magnette to the traditional TF, which still had a separate chassis and steel-clad ash-framed bodywork, much as used way back in the late 1920s on the first MG Midget.

Perhaps now we should look at the structure of BMC at that time. In 1952 the Morris and Austin empires amalgamated under the new group name of British Motor Corporation, following many years when a merger between the two giants of the British motor industry had been proposed and discussed but never carried out. Negotiations between William Morris, later Lord Nuffield, and Sir Herbert Austin had actually started as long ago as 1924 around the time the MG marque was born

At that time, the proposed merger would have also involved Wolseley; but later Morris bought this for his Nuffield Group, outbidding Herbert Austin for the business. Both men were autocratic, self-made millionaires and it is not surprising that they were unable to agree merger terms that would have reduced the control they had over their individual empires.

An early TF catalogue at pains to portray the connection of the marque with motor sport.

The British Motor Corporation inherited a large number of factories and many British car marques. The Nuffield Group, in particular, brought to the corporation widely diverse companies producing both the raw materials and the finished components needed for vehicle production. Many of these had been bought by William Morris in his search for greater control over prices and sources of supply, but were scattered geographically. The merger with Austin brought yet more manufacturing capacity, with much duplication of resources, but as a bonus, did include the benefit of Longbridge, at that time the most up-to-date car factory in the country. Under the direction of Leonard Lord, the Longbridge plant had been modernised in the early post-war years with the car assembly building being fed with components from other parts of the site via a system of underground tunnels.

As well as inheriting the production facilities from both sides, the new British Motor Corporation was now faced with a bewildering range of models, many of which were in direct competition with each other. Although billed as a merger, the real control was now vested in the younger Austin management team and it was these men who took on the task of rationalisation. The marques then represented by BMC were Austin, Morris, Riley, Wolseley and, of course, MG. In addition there were Morris Commercials and Nuffield Tractors, and from 1952 Austin-Healey, a new sports car marque introduced by Leonard Lord despite the Corporation already owning the established and respected MG brand.

The new TF alongside a Z-Magnette at the 1954 Paris Salon.

A left-hand drive TF with wire wheels photographed for publicity purposes.

A restored TF finished in the popular combination of red paintwork and tan leather seat facings with matching Rexine trim.

A TF rolling chassis.

An export TF photographed on Lambourne Downs.

In 1953 there was no design office at Abingdon and this was not re-established until 1954 when the BMC management were persuaded of the urgent need for an entirely new car. However, when the TD was redesigned to produce the TF all this was in the future and the powers that be would only sanction a facelift of the old model to be carried out by the design office at Cowley. Gerald Palmer, who at the time had overall design responsibility for MG, Riley and Wolseley, had produced a few years earlier proposals for a new MG of unitary construction but pressure of other work and shortage of money had prevented these going beyond the mock-up stage.

For an interim model, the brief given to the design team at Cowley, liaising with Syd Enever at Abingdon was to improve the appearance of the car without spending too much money and at the same time to deal with a few issues that were causing problems in service. One of these was the use of separate headlamps on the TD. These were easily damaged and knocked out of alignment by owners and by careless garage staff when opening the bonnet. These units were costly to repair and replace. Another area where the old model was showing its age was the lack of a pressurised cooling system. This was particularly important in some export markets where hot weather was the norm. However, changing it meant modifications to the design of both the header tank and the filler cap.

One has to admit that the design produced was aesthetically very successful. Basically this consisted of

A TF1250 in cream with green interior, an attractive combination.

a revised body tub with a lower scuttle that blended well with a gently sloping bonnet, which now had fixed side panels. New, beautifully sculptured front wings incorporating the smaller diameter headlight units, plus elegant running boards and chunky rear wings, as a whole produced a very attractive car. The radiator cap was now a dummy fixed at the top of the sloping radiator shell and the working filler cap for the now pressurised cooling system was accessed by raising the left-hand bonnet top. This bonnet still featured a centre hinge but now only the top panels lifted for routine maintenance. The side panels could be unscrewed for major work.

At the rear, the fuel tank was reshaped and lowered and the rear wings had a curved leading edge that was designed to blend into the running boards. The tread

One of many TF originally exported that has been repatriated in recent years and converted to right-hand drive.

Restored TF1500 finished in the correct shade of red and fitted with wire wheels.

strips on these were chrome plated, rather than made from an aluminium extrusion fitted with rubber inserts, and were now carried on higher up to end on the tops of the front wings. The circular rear lights fitted to later TDs were carried over unaltered for the TF, as were the front sidelights.

Inside, the cockpit much was new. Gone was the bench seat familiar to generations of Midget owners from the first M-type sold in 1929 to the last TD in 1953. In its place was a pair of upholstered bucket seats with leather wearing surfaces, which, although very comfortable, did not have quite the range of adjustment of the earlier arrangement. Behind the seats the side-screen stowage had been changed. On the TD the four side-screens stowed vertically in a compartment at the rear, but with the TF this compartment was moved so that they sat flat in a box carried beneath the luggage area. As with the previous

The cramped engine compartment of a TF1500 showing why the TD oil bath air cleaner had to be replaced with twin pancake filters.

A home market TF1250 looks good with the standard steel wheels and chrome hubcaps.

A BMC publicity picture with the two sports car brands, Austin-Healey and MG, in a rural location.

models, a short tonneau cover was supplied with the car to enclose the stowed hood and the luggage compartment, and this could be left in place with the side-screens fitted.

Both as a styling gimmick and to ease production of both left and right hand drive cars on the same production line, the instruments were now all grouped in the centre of the dashboard. Following the style of those that had been fitted to the now superseded Y-type saloon, these round instruments were set under chromed, octagonal bezels with the rev counter placed nearest to the driver and the speedometer on the passenger side. In the centre a combined instrument took care of water temperature, oil pressure and

To identify the more powerful version badges carrying the logo TF-1500 was fitted each side of the bonnet.

The revised cockpit and instrument panel of the TF was not as easy to use as on the TD, but was more readily assembled to suit either left-hand or right-hand drive markets.

The tool kit for a TF.

ammeter. There was still no fuel gauge, just a low fuel warning light that flashed when the remaining petrol in the tank was running low.

Either side of the instrument panel was a small open glove box that, together with the door pockets fitted to all T-types, gave sufficient useful storage for oddments. When a radio was fitted the controls were placed in one of these glove boxes and the valve amplifier was mounted under the dashboard. A modern wiper motor fixed to the scuttle replaced the unreliable and vulnerable unit mounted on the windscreen frame of the TD, and a pair of knobs inside the glove boxes was provided to park the blades clear of the windscreen. For the driver moving on from a TD the pedal positions, handbrake, adjustable steering wheel and foot-operated dipswitch fitted to later versions of that model would be familiar.

However, the changes to the exterior and interior of the car couldn't disguise the fact that the chassis and other mechanical components were pure TD. The only improvements made for the new model were the standardisation of a higher state of tune for the engine, similar to that used on the TD Mark II, and the adoption of the higher ratio rear axle from that model. The engine amendments improved the power output by a modest 4bhp. In addition, because of the restricted space under the bonnet, a pair of pancake filters replaced the oil bath air cleaner of the TD.

One important chassis change for those sports car buyers who lamented the lack of wire wheels on the TD was the adoption of these as an optional extra on the TF. They were particularly popular in overseas markets and some kits of parts were later sold to convert earlier TDs to wire wheels. The new car sold in Britain at £550 plus £230.5.10d. purchase tax, which was £20 more than the TD but £35 less than the mechanically similar, but more highly tuned, TD Mk II Midget.

The TF colour choice was similar to earlier cars: black paintwork with red, green or tan trim, red with red or tan trim, ivory with red or green trim, grey with red trim, and green with green or tan trim. On many TFs this green was a metallic finish. Black trim was never an option and tan trim was not fitted to ivory cars in spite of the number with that combination around today.

Two new TFs destined for sale in Nairobi, Kenya were part of a consignment shipped to Mombasa and are here coming off the Likoni Ferry that crossed the mouth of the harbour. The cars were driven the 300 miles to Nairobi over dirt roads that covered them with dust in the dry season and thick mud after rain. Cleaning them prior to sale was a long and expensive process.

Although they had a new MG to sell, the Publicity Department didn't exactly go out of their way to promote the car in the home market. After the initial announcement in *The Motor* and *The Autocar* magazines in 1953 no cars were made available to them for road test. Perhaps the company feared that those journals would point out how little progress over the previous model had been made in terms of comfort and performance. Even the press advertisements for MGs tended to dwell more on the new Magnette saloon than on the virtues of the TF.

Overseas magazines did test the car and on the whole liked it, particularly the styling revisions. However, although most publications were too kind to mention it, the car was beginning to look a bit dated when compared to offerings from other manufacturers tested in their pages. *Road and Track* in America was given one of the new cars to try and published a test report in March 1954. These journalists found that the performance of the TF was better than the TD, but not quite as good as the TD Mk II. They felt that the higher gearing improved the car, but that the larger carburettors were not an improvement.

The need to try to improve sales of the car, which was not really holding its own in competition with other marques, led to the development of the larger 1466cc engine introduced after some 6000 TF 1250s had been built. For some while a number of people had been enlarging the XPAG engine by over-boring. This process was not always successful as it reduced the wall thickness around the bores below acceptable limits. To enlarge the capacity without changing the cylinder bore centres, or the head stud positions, the factory produced a new block casting which eliminated the water jacket between 1 and 2 and 3 and 4 cylinders and reduced the size of the jacket between the two pairs of cylinders and at the front and rear of the block. The effect of raising the bore size from 66.5 to 72mm was to increase the capacity from 1250cc to 1466cc. The cylinder head was unchanged so the increase in swept volume meant a corresponding increase in compression ratio to 8.3:1. The power went up by a useful 6bhp and torque was also improved.

To help market the new version of the TF the factory added TF1500 plates to the sides of the bonnet. In advertisements the slogan 'There's a new bee in its bonnet!' was used to emphasise the improved performance. However, good though the new engine was, sales of the now seriously outdated car did not pick up and at the Abingdon factory the newly reformed design team were by this time hard at work on the replacement model, the streamlined MGA.

Yet one only has to see just how much interest there is in the replicas produced over the years to appreciate how well the styling has stood the test of time. To many the TF is one of the best looking of all the MGs and one that has sufficient modern improvements, rack and pinion steering, independent front suspension, more effective braking, allied to a comfortable cockpit and good ride and roadholding, to make it a car better suited to use daily.

TF1500 sales brochure.

Detail from early TF sales brochure.

TF showroom poster.

Early TF1250 sales leaflet.

TF Special Bodied Car

Only one TF rolling chassis appears to have been given specialist coachwork. LHD chassis 5015 went down the line on 22nd April 1954 and was given a chassis plate with car number 34858 inscribed. It went to Europe where it was given a body designed and built by Ghia-Monviso. It was one of a small number of cars built by them for Paris-based Sapcar and carries their badge on the sides of the front wings, alongside the Everest name. On the boot there is a chromed MG logo and above that the letters Midget TF. The car spent most of its early years in a Swiss car museum and was put up for sale in 2007 through Geneva-based Classic Car Collection. At that time there was a recorded 6307 miles on the standard TF speedometer. This had been used in the Everest, along with the other normal MG instruments, on the special dashboard. The original light metallic blue paintwork and all the interior trim remained as built. It was sold reputedly to a buyer in Ireland.

TF In Competition

As soon as the new TF Midgets were in the hands of those owners keen to use them in competition then the model began appearing in entry lists. Most of their efforts were not covered in the major motoring magazines, but events like the 1954 Welsh Rally were given space. Run by the Blackpool and Fylde Motor Club, the rally started from Chester Castle at midnight and finished 300 miles later at the Club headquarters in Blackpool. JJB 580 was a very new looking TF entered

This LHD TF was exported as a rolling chassis to be fitted with this body designed by Ghia-Monviso. It was built by them for Paris based Sapcar and carries their badge on the front wings, alongside the Everest name.

by Ted Lund, who had previously been one of three factory-supported drivers in production car races in MG TCs and TDs.

In 1955 the BMC Competition Department was formed with the aim of getting the company's cars to the top of motor sport. Based at Abingdon, the new department was headed up by Marcus Chambers with S.C.H. 'Sammy' Davis as advisor. The first event was the Monte Carlo Rally and in this three MG ZA Magnettes were joined by the same number of Austin Westminsters. Team results were a disappointment.

For the RAC Rally in March, a factory-supplied MG TF1500, driven by Pat Moss in what was her first rally, joined the team of three Monte Carlo Magnettes. Partnered by Pat Faitchney, she was placed third in class 3, the one set aside for female drivers. It was a particularly tough event with a series of night navigation runs that required precise map reading in order not to be either behind or ahead of the correct time when competitors arrived at a number of secret checks. There were also speed events at venues like Cadwell Park and Oulton Park before final tests at Blackpool. In these Pat Moss set the fifth fastest time overall and beat all others in her class. After this John Thornley let her hold onto the TF for a while so as to gain experience by taking part in a few club rallies and races.

The TF1500 was entered in a couple of handicap

This TF was privately entered in the 1955 RAC Rally.

For the 1955 RAC Rally this factory-supplied MG TF1500 driven by Pat Moss, in what was her first such event, joined the team of three Monte Carlo Magnettes. Partnered by Pat Faitchney, she was placed third in class 3. That was the one set aside for female drivers.

races at Goodwood. In the first of these she took advantage of a min 20sec handicap and led home Patsy Burt in an Aston Martin by 20sec. She was re-handicapped for the next race and could only manage sixth place. The arrival of the MGA later in 1955 meant that for the future events the Competition Department concentrated on that model and others in the BMC range.

TF Changes In Production

Mechanical

XPAG/TF/31263	Oil pump made self-priming
XPAG/TF/31943	Lower banjo coupling on oil pipe carrying oil to cylinder head had internal diameter reduced
XPAG/TF/33024	Oil suction pipe and sump modified
TF 3495	Dampers added to carburettors
TF 3811	Wire wheel cars had improved front wheel grease retainers
TF 4760	Threads on tie rod ends changed to UNF
XPEG/501	First TF 1500. Badges fitted to sides of bonnet and red reflectors to back of car
TF 6887	Wire wheels given a deeper dished inner flange
TF 6950	Last car with 1250cc engine

Following the RAC Rally, John Thornley let Pat Moss hold on to the TF for a while to gain experience by taking part in a few club rallies and races. She entered the car a couple of handicap races at Goodwood and in the first of these she took advantage of a 1 min 20 sec handicap and led Patsy Burt in an Aston Martin home by 20 sec. She was handicapped for the next race and could only manage sixth place.

Electrical

TF 1501	Fuel pump changed to SU HP-type AUA 57 mounted on special bracket fixed to rear of chassis
TF 8146	The casting for the Lucas WT618 horn changed

Specification TF

Wheelbase/track	7' 10"/Front 3' 11⅜" Rear 4' 2"
Suspension	Front Independent with coil springs and wishbones
	Rear Leaf springs
Wheels/tyres	Pressed steel with optional extra cost painted wire
Brake drum size	9 inch
Engine/power output	XPAG 1250cc/57bhp
	XPEG 1466cc/63bhp
Gearbox	4-speed synchromesh on top three ratios
Build dates	1250 model 5th October 1953 to 31st May 1954
	1500 model 13th July 1954 to 4th April 1955
Cars built	1250 Model 6200 1500 Model 3400 (including one rolling chassis)

Appendix

Notes on equipment fitted to T-series Midgets

Instruments

The speedometer and tachometer on the TA, TB, TC and early TD are chronometric instruments, and the later TD and TF are magnetic. It is very easy to see which type is used as the early instruments have flat faces and the later have a dished rim to the dial. With either type the revolution counter has a potential weakness in the gearbox on the dynamo and with the cable drive. One reason for the early failure of the gearbox is that over-tightening the securing nut cracks the casing. The instruments fitted to Midgets from the later J2 to the early TD were very similar, although the markings and colour of the dials differed. A problem with using some otherwise very similar instruments on these later cars will be fitting the 30mph warning light as the electrical contacts and external fixings were not present on earlier speedometers.

The clock fitted to the tachometer is a separate unit and this is often missing on reproduction instruments. On the TA and TB the clock mechanism was mechanical, but the later cars had an electric clock.

The supplementary instruments fitted to the TA, TB, TC and TD are easy to find as, like the larger instruments, the cases did not change for many years and old units with black dials can be used and re-painted. The TC was not fitted with a temperature gauge as standard, but many had them fitted later. These were usually mounted on the right hand side of the dashboard, outboard of the tachometer. The early TD also lacked a temperature gauge, but a dual water/oil pressure gauge was fitted from TD 13914. Although this dual gauge was not fitted to early TDs it was available to fit soon after production started. The pre-war cars really need to have a separate temperature gauge and, as an alternative, popular accessories were the thermometers that fitted to drilled radiator caps.

The ammeter changed from 20amp to 30amp when

This type of tachometer and speedometer were fitted to the TA, TB and TC. Also used up to TD 10750 left-hand drive and TD 10778 right-hand drive.

Example of the later, magnetic instruments with the dished dial fitted to later TDs.

The drive for the speedometer using a gearbox fitted to the back of the dynamo.

the TD instruments changed to magnetic. There was also a high beam warning light fitted to the speedometer from TD 17548, but these can be found on earlier cars, as all the replacement magnetic type speedometers seem to have been so fitted.

Switches

A Lucas horn and dipswitch 17A L15, part no. 380191, was used on the TA, TB, TC and TD up to TD 18882 when a separate foot-operated dipswitch was fitted. Correctly the dashboard switch sits on a flat, chromium-plated bezel and the black enamelled switch carries white lettering D and H to indicate dip or headlamps. After the separate dipswitch was fitted, the combined unit was replaced with a horn push of identical pattern but lacking the switch lever and lettering. A service sheet was issued at that point detailing the conversion of earlier cars.

The ignition and lighting switch was a Lucas PLC.

Style of headlamp used for the TA/TB and early TC models.

On TA/TB units there were four positions: Low and High charge, Side and Head lights. The lettering was recessed and filled with white paint. When a voltage regulator was fitted post-war the switch was Lucas PLC6L114, part no. 34018A, and these were fitted to all TCs and TDs. The correct type has OFF/S/H in white lettering at the top and LUCAS in white below. The switch sits in the metal centre panel and is held in place at the back with a wire clip that sits in slots cut in the side of the switch body. These slots are at various places to accommodate different thickness panels used on other vehicles. There are quite a number of variations that may have been fitted over the years. Some later types had a window with the lettering appearing as the switch was moved and are often fitted as replacements.

There was just one basic design of the centre panel, fitted to all the T-type cars from the TA to the TD, although there were quite a few differences in layout of the instruments and switches between models and also to accommodate export variations. On all the panels the raised rim was chrome plated and polished, whilst the centre was painted. The panels of the TA, TB and TC, up to approximately TC5500, were painted black with white lettering printed on them to identify the various knobs and switches. When the colour was changed to a metallic tan these had black lettering, although this detail was omitted from the EX-U version. The TD panels were all painted the tan colour without lettering.

The TF instrument panel was of a different design, but was also finished in the metallic bronze/tan colour. The control knobs on the TF were embossed with letters to identify their purpose, so no panel lettering was needed.

The pair of lamps fitted one each side of the centre panel on the TA, TB and TC models were: a map light DF41, part no. 56040A, and a 30mph warning light DF41 DA21, part no. 56042A. The TD had no lamps and the instruments were internally lit. The bases of the two lamps are identical, only the top covers differ. On the TA, TB and early TC the bases were painted black but this changed to tan when the colour of the centre panel was altered. The 30mph lamp was first introduced in the 1930s. At that time the general speed limit for urban areas in the United Kingdom was raised to 30mph. The idea was that it operated between 20 and 30mph to indicate that you were not exceeding the speed limit. This lamp was only fitted to home market cars, its place taken by a second map lamp for export models.

The PS6 L switch, part no. 314090, was used for the TA, TB, TC and TD panel lights and fog lamp. From TD10751 LHD, TD 10779 RHD, the panel light switch was changed for one incorporating a rheostat to dim the lighting if required, part no. 78405. On export TCs fitted with flashing turn indicators a switch, SD84/L18 part no. 31219A, was fitted to the centre of the instrument panel in place of the inspection lamp socket. The knobs of the starter and mixture controls on the TC are of a different shape to those of the TD. The TC knobs are of a slightly smaller diameter, with a longer stem than the TD. The TF knobs are different again, being octagonal and carrying letters to indicate their use. TDs, after TD 22315, were fitted with flashing direction indicators for some overseas markets. The instrument panel gained an extra hole in the centre for the WL3/1 warning lamp. Where this was not needed the hole was covered with a plug.

This same style of warning lamp was fitted to the EX-U TCs as a headlamp high beam warning lamp was fitted in place of the fog lamp switch, and on both TCs and TDs this space carried an ignition warning light. The TDs fitted with indicators have the self -cancelling switch, the same pattern as was used on the TF and MGA, mounted on a special bracket beneath the dashboard. The relay was Lucas part no. 33117 and was used, in conjunction with a flasher unit, to flash a second filament in the front sidelights and to interrupt the rear brake light circuit. On the TD the relay was mounted on the bulkhead in the engine compartment and to make room for it the body plate moved to the side of the bulkhead.

Other Electrical Equipment

Coil. Coil Q12L, part no. 45020A, was fitted to TA, TB, TC TD and early TF. This was painted black with a deep-red top cover. The later TFs were fitted with coil LA12, part no. 45172. These had an unpainted aluminium body and a black top cover.

Voltage regulator. The pre-war TA & TB were not fitted with a regulator but carried the Lucas CJR3L35 type cutout and fuse box with six fuses. Post-war there were three different types of regulator fitted. The early TCs had the large RF91 unit, replaced from TC 3414 by the RF95/2 part no. 37507. This latter unit was also fitted to the TD until superseded by type RB106/1 used with a separate fuse box type SF6. All of these units carried only two fuses and for the American market, TC EX-U, an extra fuse box SF5/2, part no. 37107A was fitted.

Dynamo. The TA and TB had a three-brush type C45NV2 producing both low and high rates of charge. The TC was fitted with the Lucas C45YV-3GC24, part no. 228334. The early TD used type C39PVDA41, later replaced with C39PV/2. That part continued in use with the TF. All of these had a threaded boss on which the gearbox driving the tachometer was fitted. There were many similar looking units fitted to other vehicles that were not so equipped.

Starter motor. The TA/TB unit was type M418A84. The TC had a Lucas M418G LO starter motor, part no. 255378, and starter switch ST10, part no. 763251. The TD and TF had the M35G/1L3/1, part no. 25022. This starter has 10 teeth on the pinion and will not fit a TC unless the ring gear on the flywheel is changed. The later cars had an ST19 starter switch, part no. 76701, as fitted to MGAs.

Lamps. The 8in headlamps on the TA, TB and TC built for the home market were arranged so that on dip only the nearside lamp remained lit, now no longer

The Lucas FT27 spot lamp fitted to all TAs, TBs and TCs up to chassis TC 4738.

The Lucas SFT 462 fitted from chassis TC 4739. It was also available as an extra on TDs.

legal. For export markets both lamps dipped and the later, special EX-U model was fitted with 7in S700 headlamps capable of taking sealed beam units. The early headlamps fitted to TA, TB and early TCs had a U-shaped pattern in their fairly flat lens glasses with rims that started with quite a flat section before curving over to hold the glass. The later MBD140 lamp had a much more domed lens with a diamond shape in the glass and rims that have a tighter, more uniform curve. Both types have the inset King of the Road badges and are chromed all over, except for the mounting plates, which were painted black.

TDs all had double-dipping S700 headlamps. During the production run the straight dip lamps fitted to all the early cars were replaced by units that dipped either to the right or to the left according to the market. There is a lot of doubt as to which TDs had lamps chromed all over. During production there was a period when the body of the lamp was painted, although the rim remained chromed, but details of this are sketchy. Some authorities claim that all Mark IIs had chrome headlamps but even this is uncertain. The truth may be that chromed lamps were in short supply and were fitted at random as and when they were available. TFs all had the flush-fitting F700 lamps.

From TD 21303 the rear wings were modified to accommodate this circular rear stop/tail light and chromed plinth. This type was fitted to all TFs.

Sidelights with plastic red dots on the top that indicate to the driver that they are lit were fitted to all T-types.

The front sidelights for all T-series Midgets were the chromed Lucas 1130, part no. 52030. They carried a red spot on the top as an indication to the driver when they were lit. This red plastic lens fades badly. The front glass had a rim formed around it.

TAs up to approximately chassis number 1789 had a single round tail/stop/number plate lamp, ST38, mounted on an extension to the number plate. This was chrome plated all over on most cars although on a few early examples only the rim was chromed.

Later TAs, TBs and TCs were fitted with a single Lucas ST51 D lamp, part no. 53029, incorporating tail, stop and number plate lights. This D lamp had a separating bar in the lens and was chrome plated all over. The EX-U variant was fitted with two 482/1 stop/tail lights, part no. 53131, held by brackets that positioned the lights towards the top of the sides of the petrol tank. On this model the number plate light was a 467/1 lamp, part no. 53093, which was also used for the TD and TF. Early versions of this lamp had two bulbs and the later just one. The rear stop/tail lamps for the TD were Lucas 4721 mounted on the rear wings, later replaced for TD 21303 onwards by the circular 488 stop and tail lamp mounted in the same position, but on a chromed plinth shaped to match that of the lights. These later lamps were also fitted to the TF.

The spot lamp fitted to TAs, TBs and early TCs was the FT27. From TC 4739 the lamp changed to the SFT462 and this was also available as an extra on the TD. The option available for the TF was the SFT576, often paired with the SLR576 spot lamp. The EX-U TC did not have a fog lamp as standard. Where fitted in export markets the fog lamp was moved to the other side of the badge bar if the car was to be driven on the right-hand side of the road.

Reflectors were fitted as standard on the TF1500 models and were mounted on curved rubber plinths to the sides of the body above the rear wing. Reflectors were also fitted for some overseas markets to the earlier cars.

Horn. The TA/TB horn was a Lucas Altette type HF/934/2. The TC was fitted with the Lucas HF1234 horn, which was similar to the pre-war item with a chromed outer bezel and a black crackle painted centre. The domed nuts securing the bezel and the centre ring were also chromed, with the pre-war version being fluted and more pointed than the later ones. The Lucas service instructions for this model give the current consumption as 4amps when correctly adjusted.

The TD and TF had two windtone horns type WT614. The type WT614 horns were also fitted to the EX-U TCs. The TD horns were mounted on the bulkhead, but shortage of space in the TF engine bay forced their relocation to a position below the radiator.

Fuel pump. All models up to the early TF have the low-pressure SU pump mounted on the bulkhead, while later TFs have a high-pressure pump fixed to the offside rear chassis rail. The early pumps, including on early TCs, had brass bodies, and later were of cast aluminium. The TD Mark II has twin pumps with the fuel lines duplicated right back to the fuel tank. The TA/TB petrol tap is fitted to the side of the toolbox with the control knob on the right-hand side of the dashboard.

Wiper motor. The Lucas CW1 motor was fitted to the TA, TB, TC, and the TD except for the Tickford. This motor was made for many years in 6-, 12- and 24-volt guises with the 12-volt the only one suitable for T-series Midgets. These cars use a 150-degree sweep. TDs from chassis number 22315 had the wiper motor moved to the centre of the screen. The electric 12volt feed wire for all TDs came through the scuttle on the right-hand side and was transferred to the other side of the windscreen inside the top rail for right-hand drive models.

The TF used a more modern wiper motor, Lucas CRT12, mounted on the scuttle with cable drive to the arms. These arms were brought into use by turning knurled knobs, one in each glove pocket, with the driver's side knob also switching on the motor.

Distributor. The TA, TB and TC were fitted with distributor DK4 AA35 on TA and DKY4A, DA34 on TB/TC, incorporating micrometer adjustment of the timing. This is part of the clamping bracket but is a fairly inaccurate method of adjustment. The TD/TF DKY4A at first and D2 A4, from TD 22735, did not have a micrometer adjustment but the clamp bracket changed with the change of distributor.

On the early distributor the lobes of the cam that operates the points are symmetric and from above appear almost square, with flat sides and round corners. The later high=lift model has rounded sides and the corners are very pointed. As these cams are interchangeable an early car may have the later high-lift cam. The gap for the early type is 10-12 thou and for the later 14-16 thou.

The advance curve of the distributor is determined by the springs fitted to the advance weights. With the engine running it is possible to check this with a timing light, as long as the position of the 32 degree mark is first calculated and painted on the timing cover; the setting is reduced to 24 degrees for later cars.

TF speedometer.

TF tachometer.

The smaller TF gauges for water temperature, oil pressure and ammeter are fitted in a panel that matches those for the speedometer and tachometer.

Index